Self-Employed

Self-Employed
50 SIGNS THAT
YOU MIGHT BE
AN ENTREPRENEUR

Joel Comm & John Rampton

NEW YORK

NASHVILLE • MELBOURNE • VANCOUVER

Self-Employed
50 SIGNS THAT YOU MIGHT BE AN ENTREPRENEUR

Published in New York, New York, by Morgan James Publishing. Morgan James is a trademark of Morgan James, LLC. www.MorganJamesPublishing.com

The Morgan James Speakers Group can bring authors to your live event. For more information or to book an event visit The Morgan James Speakers Group at www.TheMorganJamesSpeakersGroup.com.

ISBN 978-1-68350-173-2 paperback
ISBN 978-1-68350-174-9 eBook
Library of Congress Control Number: 2016912393

Cover Design by:
Rachel Lopez
www.r2cdesign.com

Interior Design by:
Bonnie Bushman
The Whole Caboodle Graphic Design

In an effort to support local communities, raise awareness and funds, Morgan James Publishing donates a percentage of all book sales for the life of each book to Habitat for Humanity Peninsula and Greater Williamsburg.

Get involved today! Visit
www.MorganJamesBuilds.com

Table of Contents

Foreword

For some people, the decision to start their own business is easy. They've always known that they were entrepreneurs. They started early, they succeeded quickly and they never looked back.

For other people, it's much harder. They have good jobs that are reasonably satisfying and well-paid. They have families they need to support. They're content… and yet they know that they should be doing something else. They have an idea for a product, and they're sure it would be a huge hit.

And once it's a hit, they know they'll be able to do all of the things that they've always dreamed of doing: living on their own terms, building a giant business, setting—and reaching—their own goals.

All they have to do is find the courage to take that first step.

It's not easy. It takes a special person to be an entrepreneur. That's why most people don't do it. As Joel Comm and John Rampton point out in this book, nearly two-thirds of people in their twenties say they want to run their own businesses. In practice, it will only happen for perhaps one in ten. Everyone else works for that ten percent.

So whenever anyone came before me in episodes of Shark Tank, as I assessed their product and its chances of success, I was also admiring them. Whether they walked away with a deal or not, they had won my respect. They didn't just have an idea. They also took the steps to make it happen. They planned the product, they did the research and they prepared the pitch. That's effort and determination, and it's vital.

But before doing any of that, they did something even more important.

They looked at themselves, and they decided that they were, indeed, an entrepreneur.

They were a business-builder. They were going to be the boss. They were going to set the direction, and they were going to make their vision happen.

It's courageous and it's admirable... and it's often a leap of faith because the only people who know what it really takes to be an entrepreneur are the people who have done it.

Even early employees don't understand what it takes to create a business. They come in once the funding and the pitching and the brainstorming have already happened. They live with the growth of the company but they don't see the worry and the setbacks and the networking that are a necessary part of any entrepreneur's life.

Joel Comm and John Rampton are both successful entrepreneurs. They've both built businesses, seen them rise and fall, then rise again and sold them for millions. And they've spent the last years helping other entrepreneurs make their dreams happen. They're business-builders and they network with other business-builders too.

In this book, they review fifty of the characteristics necessary to build a successful business. They look at where entrepreneurs come from and how they live. They examine who they are and how they work. They explain what they do, and as they describe the life and personality of an entrepreneur, they show all of us what it takes to turn an idea into a business, and a dream of entrepreneurship into a whole new life.

It's the closest thing we can get to understanding what it means to be an entrepreneur.

The decision to branch out on your own can be terrifying. It *should* be terrifying. Creating your own company will require patience, sacrifice, determination, a thick skin, the support of friends and family, and of course, funds. And that's before you even get round to discussing the idea.

Start here. Understand what it takes to become a business-builder, to be an entrepreneur and to employ yourself. Then get ready to make the most momentous decision of your life.

Kevin Harrington
Original Shark from TV's Shark Tank

Introduction

Entrepreneurs are a unique group of people, and also a diverse group of people. Yet, we have found that entrepreneurs seem to think differently. They act differently. They achieve differently.

They're not content to collect a paycheck, however big. They won't be satisfied with steady promotions and increased responsibility. It's not enough for them to take charge of a project and see it through to a successful conclusion.

As long as they're working for someone else, obeying instructions, seeking approval, reporting results, realizing someone else's vision instead of their own, they won't be happy.

They want it all.

They want to have the idea. They want to create the organization. They want to hire the key personnel, set the targets, oversee the design, determine the marketing strategy, and plan the growth. They want to be able to sit back when it's all over, when the product is built and the customers are happy, and say: "I did that."

They're not alone. Lots of people would like to say that. According to the results of a 2014 survey by the University of Phoenix School of Business, half of all working adults in the US either already own their own business or would like to own a business one day. That spirit seems to be strongest among the young, however there was a study done in 2014 by "Easy Life Cover," which said the amount of new entrepreneurs for the last 10 years had been over 50 years of age, and 1 in 3 people in the 55-64 age range. Other surveys have put the number of budding entrepreneurs among twenty-somethings as high as 63 percent.

But it doesn't always happen. In fact, at any one time, only about one American in ten actually does own their own business and run it full-time. The rest of the working population continues to pull a paycheck and work for someone who is an entrepreneur.

The reasons for the gap between the desire to go your own way and acting on that wish are clear to anyone who has ever gone through the process of incorporating, investing, hiring, producing and marketing.

Being an entrepreneur is hard!

It takes courage and commitment and determination. It takes knowledge and talent and connections. It takes bold decisions and an ability to bounce back when those decisions turn out to be wrong. It can take a long, long time.

We all have great ideas. We've all spotted what look like gaps in the market, thought of products that people would love and wished that someone would deliver a particular kind of service—before the light bulb goes out in our heads, and we've thought, "Well, why don't I do it?"

But that's the easy part. On any entrepreneurial journey, that initial idea might feel the most important part of the business, but that exhilarating idea moment is the moment that takes the least amount of time and effort. Entrepreneurs might have a dozen billion-dollar ideas before breakfast.

It's not enough for an entrepreneur to be an original thinker. They also have to be unstoppable doers. They have to be able to find people, employ them and motivate them. They have to be able to raise the funds, be willing to risk the money they find, and put in all the hours and mornings and weekends, and holidays they need to turn the vision in their heads into something that other people can see and use and enjoy.

The idea is the inspiration that makes up the 1 percent of the success in every successful business; what remains is the perspiration and the organization—and there's a lot of both in every successful business.

There is no greater challenge than creating and running your own business. And for an entrepreneur, there is no greater satisfaction.

But it's not for everyone. It's for people who were born to do it, people who couldn't do anything but run their own business—not just talk about it or say they want to do it, but people who actually feel that uncontrollable drive to make something happen, and who eventually embrace that urge and harness it.

That's what this book is about. It's about what it actually takes to be an entrepreneur. It's about the passion that forces entrepreneurs to draw up yet another business plan and the determination that has them preparing yet another product launch. It's about the behavior patterns that entrepreneurs follow and the sacrifices they make to reach their goals.

We wrote it because we both meet lots of entrepreneurs—and lots of people who want to be entrepreneurs. We see them at the business conferences we address, we chat with them on planes and we field questions from friends and relatives who are thinking of starting their own companies. Those people aren't just looking for practical advice. They aren't just wondering what they need to do to create their own firm. They're also asking a second, unspoken question: "Is this for me? Am I really an entrepreneur? Or am I going to find myself overwhelmed, struggling and keen to return to the workplace?"

We've all witnessed that happen. We've all seen people dreaming of running their own business but who not only will never do it but who wouldn't be happy if they did. What would make them happy might be a different job, a smaller company, a change of career. But the stresses of being their own boss just wouldn't suit them.

And, we've also seen, people who might have struggled in school or in the workplace, start tinkering in their garage in their spare time, hem and haw for months and finally throw in their day job. Before anyone has noticed they're running a booming company that they're about to sell for a giant sack of cash.

We know those people because we are those people.

We're both entrepreneurs. We've both created successful businesses and grown those businesses and later sold them for millions of dollars. We've hired and developed, produced and launched, and marketed and grown. We've both had great ideas, seen them blossom and then watched a few of them crumble when they turned out to be not-so-good ideas after all. We've both made mistakes (lots of them), learned from them, and wondered whether we should throw in the towel, but came back and created something even bigger and better. We both have a list of fantastic, top-selling products and highly successful companies that we've created, and we've both dedicated ourselves to helping other entrepreneurs rise to the top. Right now, we're back on top with our startups, and actively turning them into highly profitable, rapidly expanding businesses.

In this book, we take a look at the characteristics that make up the entrepreneurs that we've met and that define our own experiences and personalities. We found fifty of those characteristics and divided them into six categories.

Background explores where entrepreneurs come from—those traits that separate an employee from an owner, a manager from a founder are often revealed early in life. They might come from family or exhibit themselves in college. They might be revealed in first jobs, and they might be seen in first attempts at business. Whatever the case, those signs are often there in the background, and every entrepreneur knows them.

No entrepreneur ever succeeds alone. The **people** who surround them and the way they relate to those people, whether they're friends or family, are often a good sign of the entrepreneurial success they're about to enjoy.

Part 2 explores those personal relationships and what they mean for entrepreneurs.

Part 3 is all about you: your **personality**, your character, your ambition and your drive. It takes a special kind of person to be an entrepreneur. In this section we look at what kind of person that is, and explore how the way you *think and act* reveals the way you'll work.

Running a business is the ultimate test of management, so Part 4 is all about **process**. It's about what entrepreneurs do and how they do it. Entrepreneurs see the big picture. They don't just *take* responsibility— they understand *why* someone *has* to take responsibility. The entrepreneur puts in place workflows that ensure that eventually, they'll be able to take pride in their work and the eventual success it will bring.

Goals for entrepreneurs are very different from those of employees, even senior-level executives. Everyone wants to succeed. Everyone wants to reach the top, achieve all they can and win the respect of their friends and family. But entrepreneurs want to change the world, and to do it in a number of different ways. This is what we'll explore in Part 5.

And, in the final part, while the **lifestyle** of a successful entrepreneur might include fast cars, secluded beaches and private jets, getting there often involves battles over power outlets in local cafes, piles of t-shirts and a home that's as much an office as a place to relax. The way you live now, even as you're striving for your own success, says much about your fit for life as an entrepreneur.

The points in each of these sections aren't meant to be checklists. No entrepreneur has all of these fifty points. Some may have done the exact opposite: neither Mark Zuckerberg nor Bill Gates completed their bachelors' degrees at Harvard, preferring to go straight into business, but Warren Buffet has a Master of Science in economics and Jeff Bezos has two bachelors' degrees in electrical engineering and computer science. Not fitting one of these points doesn't discount your entrepreneurial ambition. There are always exceptions and you could be an outlier.

Every entrepreneur has *some* of these points and each one of them has something to teach about what it takes to build, run and grow a business. As you read through the sections of this book, you might nod your head or shake it, but you should always be filling your head with the parts here that can help you.

We are hoping that you will be coming away with a better of understanding of the entrepreneurs who build our economy—and that you might just be joining this group on your way to making the world a better place—all while being self-employed.

Part 1

Background

Temper Thompson's parents own a coffee shop. They're happy running their own small business, working for themselves and serving their regular customers. They've always been helpful and loving and supportive of their son, but as he grew up, Temper wanted to do more than own a single café. He too now runs his own business, selling online courses on Kindle Publishing. In 2016, when Temper Thompson turned 18, that business was bringing in around $30,000 a month.

Entrepreneurs come from a host of different backgrounds. Some were inspired to take up their own business after seeing how much their parents enjoyed their own independence. They were able to learn from them and be mentored by them. They grew up knowing the value of entrepreneurship.

Other entrepreneurs develop that urge for independence by themselves, sometimes after seeing their parents hunt for work and battle under unappreciative managers. But, whether entrepreneurs are born or made, that drive can often be seen early: in schoolyard trades, in sidewalk lemonade stands, and in garage-based start-ups.

Often, that drive doesn't work well within the traditional workplace, so entrepreneurs sometimes struggle while they're learning the industry or building professional experience. Many entrepreneurs, like Steve Jobs, Mark Zuckerberg and Bill Gates—the business world's most famous dropouts—failed to make it all the way through college. Others finish college but can't hold down a job, while some struggle to show their skills on their résumés and interviews. For them, entrepreneurship is often the inevitable alternative to unemployment.

There are lots of different ways into the life of an entrepreneur. In this section, we explore some of the most common routes that take people into the world of their own business.

1

You Were Raised
by Entrepreneurs

W hen Ralph Lauren's daughter was six, he told her that he wanted to name a perfume after her. It's the sort of thing that dad's who own global fashion brands do for their little girls, and most would have been thrilled to see an elegant bottle of scent carrying their name in cosmetics stores around the world. Dylan had other ideas.

"No, thanks," she told her billionaire dad. "I'm saving my name for something I make myself."

Dylan Lauren is now the owner of Dylan's Candy Bar, a chain of boutique candy stores with outlets in exclusive locations across the country, including in New York, East Hampton and Miami Beach. Its flagship store in New York City is a top tourist attraction and welcomes over 2.5 million visitors every year.

Dylan Lauren is not the only child of an entrepreneur who has gone on to build their own successful business. Tom Yeardye was a stuntman and actor who teamed up with Vidal Sassoon to create a chain of hair salons. Years later, his daughter, Tamara Mellon recovered from being fired from Vogue to partner with a shoe designer called Jimmy Choo. Together, they created a fashion brand now valued at over a billion dollars.

When Jack Abraham sold Milo.com, a shopping comparison site, to eBay for $75 million in 2010, he was following in his dad's footsteps. Magid Abraham is the founder and CEO of comScore, a two-billion dollar analytics company.

The leaders of successful businesses are filled with founders who are themselves the offspring of people who created successful businesses. A 2015 study called "Why Do Entrepreneurial Parents Have Entrepreneurial Children?" found that having parents who are entrepreneurs increases the probability of the children being entrepreneurs by as much as 60 percent.

Some of that success may be down to talent. The kinds of skills necessary to succeed as an entrepreneur—a sharp mind, a willingness to take risks, a cool head, drive and management skills—may be hereditary in the same way that height and eye color are hereditary; we take aspects of our personality from our parents in the same way that we might take our mother's hair color or our father's male pattern balding.

But researchers Matthew J. Lindquist, Joeri Sol and Mirjam Van Praag, who investigated the link between entrepreneurial parents and their go-getting children, found little difference in the success rates of natural and adopted children growing up in families whose parent ran their own businesses. You might have a better chance of inheriting an entrepreneur's personality if your birth parents are entrepreneurs but success in business isn't genetic.

Something else happens as the children grow up.

That something is likely to include phone calls and check-signing. Some of the success of an entrepreneur's offspring can certainly be attributed to the ability of a rich parent to smooth the paths for their kids. Tamara Mellon's seed funding came from her father. Dylan Lauren's list of influencers includes fashion A-listers like David Beckham, Janet Jackson, Oprah Winfrey and Michelle Obama—people her father can call, but the rest of us can only read about in gossip magazines.

Certainly, when you have a rich parent who can   pay   your bills, save you the chore of pitching to venture capitalists, and can connect you to the people who can give you expertise and influence, life as an entrepreneur is always going to be a great deal easier.

But it's not only about cash and influence. What really makes the difference, say researchers, is role modeling.

Children growing up in a household in which at least one parent heads their own business will see what running a business involves. They hear the conversations about design and marketing, and get to listen to the reasons behind the decisions that founders have to make every day. For the children of entrepreneurs, life means living with a business mentor who's always available, never more than a phone call away, and wants nothing more than to see their children succeed as much as they have.

You could forget about reading the biographies of great business leaders; you'd have the life of a great business leader unrolling right next to you in real time every day.

That's a huge advantage, and it's only available to the children of entrepreneurs.

If one of your parents is an entrepreneur, there's a great chance that you're going to be one, as well—not just an entrepreneur yourself—but one as successful as your parents. You can learn from them, seek their advice and copy the strategies that they've implemented.

However, if neither parent is an entrepreneur you can still capture some of those entrepreneurial benefits and thoughts through other types of activities for which your parents are participating. An example might be seeing a parent get up everyday and go to work—no matter what, and sometimes working late or traveling and speaking at work engagements. Entrepreneurs tend to need that type of mental dedication to work, as well.

My mom (John) worked with the board of a charity for a children's hospital. The commitment took work nearly every day of the year for 25 years. She had us (her children) run all over the city to pick up needed items and deliver others. We worked in the background of the major fundraising event of the year. My mom also worked another charity that took one full day every week and she spoke at an event once a month that required visual aides—and there was no PowerPoint in those days. Guess who helped with the visuals for that?

The case with neither of our families being what would be called a traditional entrepreneur, as the word is defined now, doesn't mean you don't have examples you can draw from. We both had hard-working parents that encouraged us to start working for money at an early age. This meant paper routes, moving lawns and lemonade stands, followed by getting outside part-time jobs as soon as we could, (and still keeping the paper route on the side).

So, besides both of our parents having a strong work ethic, they instilled other things in us, too, including how to save and spend money wisely. We were both taught to always be looking ahead for opportunities to make money—and what a difference a good income can make in your life—but also—what can happen in terms of both the benefits and the risks.

Even if you have no entrepreneurial family members, you can still become one by reaching out to others. Find a mentor. Get close to an entrepreneur that you admire, and ask if you can pepper them with questions and seek their advice. If you can use your contacts to find someone close—perhaps a friend of your parents or the parents of a friend—that's even better.

Remember that, although the chances of being an entrepreneur are higher if your parents are entrepreneurs themselves, not every son and daughter of a founder wants to go into business; some might want to be doctors, lawyers, designers or writers. And parents who are not entrepreneurs also have skills and knowledge that they want to pass on.

If your parents are entrepreneurs, there's a good chance you'll be an entrepreneur. If they're not entrepreneurs, find a mentor and entrepreneur who wants a protégé and use them as a sounding board to add business knowledge to the love and support you get from your parents.

2

You're A Drop-Out

The announcement made at Techcrunch Disrupt in 2010 was an earthquake. The event is meant to overturn convention and change industries. It's designed to launch young technology entrepreneurs, throwing funds at them and putting them on a path to the "Three Comma Club." But, when investor Peter Thiel stood up and announced that he would be giving $100,000 each, to twenty entrepreneurs under the age of twenty provided they dropped out of school, gave up on college and used the money to build a business—it was a giant poke in the eye to the education establishment.

"Don't bother with college," he was telling young entrepreneurs. "It's got nothing to teach you. Stop wasting your time and go build your company."

It's a message that many of the world's most successful entrepreneurs have delivered—not with a speech—but with their feet. Both Bill Gates and Mark Zuckerberg gave up places at Harvard, the world's most prestigious university, to take a risk with companies that could have failed. They both became billionaires.

Steve Jobs failed to graduate from Reed College, a small liberal arts school where he ended up auditing typography classes as he played around with computers and dreamed of launching Apple. More recently, Blake Mycoskie, founder of Toms Shoes, left Southern Methodist University after an injury stopped him playing tennis. He launched a campus laundry service that racked up more than a million dollars in sales before he sold it and started his new company.

Some of the world's great business-builders didn't even finish high school. David Karp, who sold Tumblr to Yahoo for over a billion dollars, left school at fifteen. Richard Branson lasted only a year longer, and Kirk Kerkorian gave it all up in the eighth grade before going on to buy a chunk of land in Vegas and own large stakes in properties including the Bellagio, Luxor and MGM Grand.

If you've gone to college, become disillusioned, then tossed away the books to launch your own firm, you're in good company. There's no shortage of founders of enormous businesses, and other business talent who have done the same thing, then gone on to do great things. Do note, however, that the non-college education trend has become less successful in recent years. In our own experience, we have found that many talented successful individuals not having a college degree has not been the end of the world for them.

However, that isn't my recommendation. It is surprising how many times that little piece of paper that says you graduated from university will open doors for you when nothing else will. If you don't have that opportunity for a university education, or you don't want it, you can still get out there and prove you can build something without having to spend hours in the classroom. With your education or whether you choose another path—we have found the most important action for an entrepreneur is to be out there, pounding the pavement, using street smarts, and experiencing what the real world has to offer.

However, it's not quite as simple as saying some entrepreneurs can't or don't complete college or that if you want to build a successful business, you need to give up your education. In 2014, LinkedIn's Data team took funding data from Crunchbase, and analyzed the demographics and relationships of more than 1,200 tech entrepreneurs whose companies had managed to raise money the previous year. What they found suggested that, if you were looking to raise funds for a tech company in 2013, it paid to not only complete college—but to attend a good one; then after university to first work and build experience at a large firm; and to wait until you're in your thirties before going cup-in-hand to investors.

Most of the VC-backed entrepreneurs had listed a college education on their LinkedIn profiles, with nearly 30 percent graduating from a top-tier school such as Stanford, MIT or Harvard. A similar percentage had worked for a company with a market capitalization of more than $50 billion, and 40 percent had worked at director-level or higher. A fifth had founded a previous company and the amount of first round funding raised increased as the age of the entrepreneur moved through their thirties.

So, if you're studious and committed to your studies or if you lacked the confidence when you were in your early twenties to break out on your own, you may still be not just an entrepreneur, but a successful one with a better chance of persuading a venture capitalist to open his wallet. Top entrepreneurs who *did* stick around at school include Jeff Bezos who picked up two bachelor's degrees from Princeton; Nick Woodman who studied visual design and creative writing at the University of California at San Diego before creating GoPro; and Jennifer Hyman, co-founder of Rent The Runway, who completed both her bachelor's degree and her MBA at Harvard where she also met her business partner.

The willingness of some top entrepreneurs to give up a good education tells us nothing about the value of education. It tells us everything about how entrepreneurs see risk.

In an interview with the BBC, Bill Gates explained his decision to leave Harvard as an easy one to make and an easy one to explain to his parents. He and Paul Allen felt that as they were studying an opportunity was opening in the new computer industry, and they were going to be left behind. "And it wasn't as though Harvard wouldn't have taken me back," he added.

If Microsoft hadn't landed some early deals, if IBM hadn't started using Windows in its machines or if Apple had devoted as much time to software as it was dedicating to hardware, Bill Gates could simply have returned to Harvard and continued his studies, a little more experienced and a little better able and ready to face the world upon graduation.

Entrepreneurs make difficult decisions every day. They have to decide how to invest their resources, which features need to be cut to bring the product out on time, and which benefits to emphasize in their marketing. They have to choose personnel to lead projects, define corporate messages and make deals with partners, suppliers and distributors that will make or break the company. The choice to forego parts of an education is just one decision that an entrepreneur has to make. What makes someone an entrepreneur isn't the difficult decision they make, but their willingness to make it.

Though we can all name that handful of incredible, famous, and not-formally-educated entrepreneurs—what are the other entrepreneurs doing? Well, most of them have gotten their education and finished university. We both finished college. I (Joel), while a seasoned keynote speaker, have surprisingly never used my degree in Speech Communications from University of Illinois to secure a job. So have our degrees helped us be entrepreneurs? We can't say for sure. The actual studies didn't really help, but here is what *did* help—life experience interacting with people as we made our transition into the real world. We learned what productivity looked like.

We discovered who the movers and shakers of the future were. We observed our professors and asked if they gave ludicrous and absurd amounts of homework? Was it a waste of time? Well, an entrepreneur learns really quickly at college that they want to be the boss. Is that a waste of time? An entrepreneur learns really quickly at college how to work and how to "please" the professors to get the grade. Is that beneficial for business? You may want to ask yourself, who will you be pleasing as an entrepreneur? Not just yourself. You will have customers (maybe even an old professor) who wants something different from your product or service, and you learn how to iterate and pivot to save your business.

There is an incredible entrepreneur we know. No one has it together like she does. Her business is worth a lot. She may not exactly be Elon Musk, but she has achieved very close to that sort of accomplishment personally, professionally and financially. She has two Ph.D.'s. She believes education is *so* important that she has set aside a million dollars (separately) for each of her grandchildren—which they will receive upon completion of a higher degree than a Bachelor's Degree. Dropping out doesn't mean you are going to succeed or fail as an entrepreneur. But, it sure could be a sign that you were made for something different.

3

You've Been Fired

There are few moments worse than when a head appears around the office door or over the top of the cubicle, and you're called into the manager's office. You know what's coming. You can see it in the manager's eyes, the way they shift in the seat, and the way they try to avoid looking at you.

You know you're being laid off.

They'll give you a reason: the company is in trouble and has to make cutbacks; you haven't met your targets; your position is being phased out; they just don't think the job suits you.

It's always painful. It doesn't matter how little you liked the job, how much you might have complained about it, and how often you might have dreamed of walking into that very office and telling your manager where he can stick his job—when the rejection is aimed in your direction, it hurts.

The only moment worse is the one that comes when you return home and have to tell your family that your job's gone. That hurts even more. Been there. Done that.

But being fired is a part of life, and it's a part of life that even many of the most successful people in the world go through at some stage. Oprah Winfrey had what she thought was her dream job reading the evening news on Baltimore WJZ-TV. That was until she was canned for becoming too emotionally involved in the stories she was describing. She was moved to daytime television, a shift that she saw as a step down until her ratings went through the roof.

Anna Wintour was fired from her position as a junior fashion editor at Harper's Bazaar because her shoots were seen as too edgy. She went on to become Vogue's most iconic editor. Even Walt Disney was shown the door at the Kansas City Star on the grounds that he "lacked imagination and had no good ideas."

All of those leaders used that one step back to give themselves a more powerful run-up before their next great leap towards the success they were destined to enjoy.

Other leaders have been fired after achieving success. Whenever entrepreneurs accept money from investors, they give themselves bosses. They have people who monitor what they do, and hold them accountable. They're no longer entirely free. The corporate world is filled with entrepreneurs who set up companies, built them, took them public and were then ousted in a boardroom coup.

Steve Jobs called being fired from Apple the best thing that could have ever happened to him. "It freed me to enter one of the most creative periods of my life," he said. He created NeXT and Pixar before returning to Apple, a little older, a little more experienced and better ready to take the computer company in a whole new direction.

Sandy Lerner, one of the founders of Cisco, got that office call shortly after Don Valentine bought 30 percent of the company for $2.6 million. Shareholders kicked Mike Lazaridis and Jim Balsillie out of Research in Motion, makers of Blackberry phones and the company they had founded. They've since become leaders in quantum computing and quantum physics.

No one is immune from being fired. From the President to the pizza delivery boy, anyone can find themselves out on their ear at any time. Even if you don't have a boss and have managed to avoid the supervision of shareholders, the moment you forget that disappointed customers have canned more entrepreneurs than any manager in history has or will, is the moment your position starts to wobble.

And, customers don't write severance checks.

Being fired is never just the end. For someone who wants to build a career, it's an opportunity to find the role that suits them best. For an entrepreneur, it's a reminder that they're not doing what they should be doing. It's the time to reflect on what you would have done differently and what you will change the next time around.

We're all put on this planet for a reason. We all have our own roles to fill and our own goals to achieve. We might all want to run the winning touchdown in the Super Bowl but that's not an achievement that we're all going to enjoy. You might think everyone wants to be the regional sales manager for your current employer, but if it's not happening, you have to ask yourself whether it's really the job for you. Whenever we try to put ourselves in a position that's not the one to which we're best suited we're only going to feel rejection and disappointment.

If you're an entrepreneur, getting laid off from a job isn't just likely. It might even be inevitable. Entrepreneurs can make great people but sometime make for bad employees. Not all the time of course, but sometimes. That difficult chat is actually a good chat because the alternative is far worse.

An entrepreneur who has never been fired, who has always managed to do a job that doesn't suit them just well enough to keep hold of it, has a big challenge. They have to find the courage to give up something easy and reliable for the difficult and risky life of a business-builder. That's the hardest career decision anyone ever has to make.

Being fired is always a powerful message that you were heading in the wrong direction. In the short term, it might be painful, even devastating if you have bills to pay, a family to feed and no financial cushion. But those difficult months will pass and in the long term, you'll look out of the window on the top floor of your own office building one day, and tell yourself, as Steve Jobs did, that being fired was the best thing that could have happened to you. It picked you up off the wrong road, turned you around and set you on the path you were always supposed to take.

Learn more about some of the times where I almost got fired and what I did to fix the situation at www.selfemployed.com/book to give you a few more practical tips to do this.

4

No One Will Give You A Job—
And That's Just Fine

When Lisa M. Blacker left medical school, she couldn't find any job let alone one in her field. Writing on Entrepreneur.com, she explained that she did what "any entrepreneur would do," and started her own business. She consulted for her former schoolmates and taught them how to market on social media.

That shift from jobseeker to entrepreneur is not unusual. More than eight million jobs were lost during the Great Recession, but as workers were receiving their pink slips and jobseekers were struggling to find positions, the rates of entrepreneurship spiked. According to a 2013 study based on data supplied by U.S. Bureau of the Census and the U.S. Bureau of Labor Statistics, the number of new businesses that opened in 2006 (the year before the recession) fell. That number rose in 2007, shot up sharply in 2008 and peaked in 2009 to reach a figure 17 percent higher than in 2006. The pattern of rising entrepreneurship matched the rise that occurred between 2001 and 2004 after the dotcom bust. Across the 250 metropolitan areas the study examined higher local unemployment rates correlated with higher rates of entrepreneurship.

Jobseekers struggle to find work for all sorts of reasons, and it's always disheartening. Every résumé that racks up a rejection feels like a personal blow. Every interview that results only in a handshake and a "Thanks for coming" sounds like someone saying, "Yeah, we don't think you're as good as you *think* you are." We all know that rejection is a part of life. We all know that everyone has the door closed in their face sometimes, that even the most successful people in the world will have applied for a job, pitched for funds, or demonstrated a product only to be told that the company thinks it's found someone or some company that's better. Knowing that rejection is inevitable doesn't make it any less painful. Rejection always hurts—and it hurts everyone in exactly the same way.

It's what happens next that makes the difference between an entrepreneur and everyone else.

Someone who has no desire to open their own company, no drive to take their own ideas and run their own business, goes in one of three directions. Most persist. They keep sending out their résumés, keep asking friends on LinkedIn, keep browsing the wanted ads. Eventually, maybe once the economy recovers, they land a position that enables them to pay the bills, even if it's not the job they dreamed of doing. For graduates who enter the labor market in a recession, it can take as long as a decade before their earnings reach the levels of people who graduated in better times.

Other jobseekers take temporary or part-time work. They move from the unemployed to the underemployed. You can see them greeting shoppers at Walmart and helping out at mail sorting offices in the run-up to Christmas. These aren't jobs that give teenagers independence and their first paychecks; these are tasks that fill a financial need for people who have the skills and experience to do so much more.

It's only better than the third way out, which is to give up. Over the last thirty years, even as medicine has advanced and legislation has made it harder for businesses to refuse work to the disabled, applications for disability benefits have reached record levels. In 1985, when the unemployment rate was a little over 7 percent, fewer than one eligible worker in a hundred applied for disability payments. In 2010, when the unemployment rate almost touched 10 percent, the percentage of workers claiming that they were too ill to ever work again had doubled. Some 14 million Americans now collect disability checks from the government instead of a pay check from an employer.

Clearly, some of those people will have needed help in any era. But when disability applications rise and fall in line with unemployment rates, it's clear that many people who struggle and fail to find work give up. They give up on life, and they give up on themselves. They decide that they'll never again receive a job that they can do, and settle for a life of no achievement and minimum and often a devastating income.

For entrepreneurs, that never happens.

In a thread on Reddit about the difficulties of job seeking, one user described himself as the "un-hirable man." Ten years in a band had left him with no education, no work experience and tattoos on his hands and face. He set up his own restaurants, took the advice of Robert Kiyosaki, author of *Rich Dad, Poor Dad*, and now describes himself as "rich."

Another user described being an unemployed single dad in 1994, looking after his four-year-old daughter. Stuck at home, he started playing with computers and the Internet. He began an SEO business, moved into paid search and twenty years later employed 150 full-time workers. When the student visa of one of his employees was about to expire, his company sponsored her, enabling her to remain in the country instead of returning to Africa.

Even entrepreneurs who should have little trouble finding work discover that their entrepreneurial spirit can kick in when they fail to land exactly the job they want. A report in *Business Insider* described how Daniel Saks struggled to find work at a Wall Street bank despite having a degree in accounting and finance from Harvard University. The recession was well under way when he graduated in 2009 and the banks that would have previously guaranteed him a lifetime of high earning were laying people off, not taking people on. Even the 100-year-old furniture firm owned by his family had just closed down. Instead of settling for underemployment and taking a job that didn't offer him the challenge he wanted, Daniel set up AppDirect, a software company that makes app marketplaces. By 2015, the company was valued at $600 million.

Jobseekers need to prove to an employer that they have the skills necessary to successfully perform a specific task. But entrepreneurs have skills that enable them to build their own success. They have drive. They have vision. They solve problems. They inspire others. They can see the big picture. When you have those life skills, you don't need to impress an employer; you are the employer.

5

You Had a Lemonade Stand—And Tried To Sell The Franchise Rights

When he was 15-years old, Richard Branson's headmaster suggested that he and his friend Jonny Gems set down their views about education in the school magazine. Branson wasn't keen on the idea. He believed that the schools' opinion about corporal punishment, compulsory chapel, sports and learning Latin were too radical for *The Stoic*. He wanted to set up his own publication that would tackle issues common across different schools.

That's where the ambitions of many bright students often reach: they think about creating their own newspaper or magazine, and they plan the sections they want to include. That's often as far as they go.

The kids who are entrepreneurs actually do it.

They write the stories and persuade their friends to contribute their own. They lay out the written material, set up and print the pages, and most likely, an entrepreneur will even manage to persuade a few businesses to place in some advertising. It's not surprising that the teenager who would soon launch a mail order business, then a record store before going on to open an airline and run a railway, picked advertisers from the telephone book, wrote to a newspaper chain about distribution and produced a real business plan for his kids' newspaper.

We can often see entrepreneurship early in life. People who have that drive to build something great, construct a company, offer a product that other people want, and make their own money --tend to show that drive early in their lives. Temper Thompson started online marketing when he was in eighth grade. Determined to make enough money to pay for his own video game habit and unwilling to ask his parents for cash, he set himself the goal of earning $100 a month. The courses that he was selling about Kindle publishing were earning him $360,000 a year when he was just seventeen.

Other teenage entrepreneurs include Leanna Archer who first turned her grandmother's hair pomade recipe into a line of natural hair products when she was nine years old. Robert Nay was fourteen when he taught himself coding, wrote Bubble Ball and generated more than a million downloads within two weeks of launch, knocking Angry Birds off its perch as the App Store's most downloaded free game. Nick D'Aloisio was just seventeen when Yahoo bought his news summary app Summly for $30 million.

One of the biggest differences between entrepreneurs and others isn't the idea. It's the execution, and that ability not just to think but to turn a plan into a product can be seen at a very young age. If you've ever sold baseball cards in the schoolyard or made your own beaded necklaces that your friends were willing to buy then you don't need anyone to tell you whether you're an entrepreneur.

In my own experiences as an entrepreneur, a severe accident that crushed my foot and ankle on a construction job site took away my ability to walk. So, while I was bed-ridden, my entrepreneurial spirit took over and I taught myself everything there was to know about Internet Marketing. I spent hours studying the market and learning how it all worked, which helped me start what turned out to become a seven-figure blog. It was this drive and determination at a young age that fueled entrepreneurial success later on. While it wasn't my first attempt at a startup business, it was the most advanced and one that I built from my original paper route and lemonade stand early days.

It seems the most traditional first business has always been the lemonade stand. It is simple to set up, easy to understand and fun to manage. A table selling a soft drink can get any young entrepreneur excited. For any parent, there are few moments more inspiring than watching their child start to fantasize about the money they're about to make. It's their first contact with being an entrepreneur—and they're thrilled! They listen when you explain about the costs of the cups, the lemons and the sugar. They toss around ideas about the size of the sign and the choice of location. They start to spread the word about their stand among their friends using social media apps that just weren't around when you were a kid. If this was you, you'll remember the pride you felt when you saw those dollar bills sticking out of the sides of your metal box.

Local news outlets, though, are now filled with stories about the police shutting down pop-up businesses that breach local laws. In the summer of 2015 they even came for Jerry Seinfeld. Or rather for his wife, Jessica, who had set up a lemonade stand in East Hampton to raise funds for a charity that helps families under financial strain. The police, acting on a neighbor's complaint, informed her that local codes in East Hampton Village forbid all peddling on village property. [I just have to comment here, that reading over this manuscript for the 20th time—I have to add this little commentary—I get sad, and even a little mad, that some idiot Hampton neighbor felt it was their crotchety duty to complain about a Lemonade stand. Oh yeah, entrepreneurs have little patience for morons, idiots and killers of dreams. We even have a few other savory words for use on "those types" of people, which probably shouldn't be added to this book.] Lemonade stands have now bumped up against local codes requiring business permits, peddler's permits and food permits, so often that campaigners declared August 10, 2013—Lemonade Freedom Day.

It's possible to exaggerate those incidents. We hear when a lemonade stand is broken up by big guys with nightsticks; we don't hear when a couple of kids get through a few gallons of lemon water and sugar undisturbed, earning enough to buy themselves a new video game.

And these days, kids have more choices. Apps like Hopscotch, Scratch and CodeMonkey are teaching children to become geeks before becoming teenagers. But, acquiring those coding skills is one thing. Turning them into a business is much harder. A 2009 study by the Pew Research Center found that just 4 percent of people aged between 16 and 29 are self-employed. The median age of first-time entrepreneurs is actually 43, a time when skills and experience have been built up, networks connected, and some capital has been accumulated.

A child who establishes any kind of business, whether it's a soft drink stand, a Minecraft live stream or a Minecraft competitor is showing exactly the drive, determination and action that makes up any entrepreneurial effort. They are going to go on to run their own business one day.

If you skipped the lemonade stand and went straight into the workplace, don't sweat it. You might not be the next Richard Branson, but record stores aren't what they used to be either, and these days setting up a business can take a lot more than a business plan and a bag of lemons.

Part 2

People

No one ever builds a business alone. They look for partners to help them get started and see them over the obstacles. They employ freelancers and staff to complete the tasks that they can't do, or to do them faster so that they can focus on the tougher jobs that they have to do alone.

Mostly, they surround themselves with people who can supply the emotional and intellectual support they need. Entrepreneurs have families who understand the sacrifices necessary to turn an idea into a business, and they appreciate the love and support their families provide.

They're sociable and capable of turning strangers into friends and colleagues, customers and partners. They might be introverted or extroverted but when they need to, they're capable of turning on the charm, talking with passion about their business and listening with clear interest to other people's stories.

They know that not everyone gets it. They understand that some people will always try to bring them down or hold them back. Not everyone will believe in their idea and those that do believe in the idea won't always think that they're the right person to make it happen. People can be destructive and cynical as well as supportive and helpful. Successful entrepreneurs know how to filter out the envious and the negative from the positive and the encouraging, to ignore the first and embrace the second.

Businesses depend on the right people. They rely on the right people in the firm, and they look to the right people outside the firm, cheering them on. In this section, we look at nine ways an entrepreneur's relationship to other people defines their chances of success.

6

You Put Your Business
Before Your Family

The biggest difference between an entrepreneur and an employee is the hours they work. Or, rather, it's the way they count the hours they work.

Ask any employee—even a high-level executive—how many hours they put in each week and they'll be able to give you pretty good ballpark figure. Someone who clocks in and out every day might know that they do exactly forty hours, unless there's some overtime going on. An executive who's paid by performance rather than by the numbers on the counter might come to a figure closer to fifty or even sixty hours in a week if they feel they're spending almost every waking hour answering emails and preparing reports.

But, ask an entrepreneur how many hours they work and you'll just get a funny look. You may as well ask them how many hours they spend breathing. For entrepreneurs there is no difference between living and working. The business fills every hour available. When they're not in the office, they're working at home. When they eat, their mobile phone is a steady serious of pings and miniature stats sheets. Even when they're driving, the one moment they can't look at a screen, they'll either be managing phone calls, listening to podcasts, or thinking about all the tasks they have to do when they reach the office, or when they get home from the office. For an entrepreneur, life is work and work is life, and they wouldn't have it any other way.

Except that life isn't work. Life is also friends and family and activities and hobbies and interests and children and all of the other things that give us a reason for doing the things that we do, and which influence the things that we do.

One of the first thing that happens when you set up your own business and start to build it is that all of those other things get pushed to one side. The business fills up all the space available.

When that means you spend less time on the surfboard or watching television, it's a pretty good exchange. You're swapping one fun activity for an even more enjoyable and valuable activity. But when it means you're spending less time with your partner or your family, it's not just you making the sacrifice.

Your partner gets to see less of you, and has to do more of the household chores that you're too busy to pick up. Your kids have one fewer play partner, and soon feel that they don't have first place in your heart. For an entrepreneur with a family, the sacrifices go beyond money and beach time and security. They're serious and they hurt.

Rand Fishkin, CEO of SEOmoz, described what those sacrifices look like in *Startup Life: Surviving and Thriving in a Relationship with an Entrepreneur*. His long work hours didn't give him the time to sleep or rest or recover from illness, so a minor cold hung around for seven weeks. His back pain was near constant and required him to walk with a cane. A "vacation" was a day on which he worked for less than four hours, and the longest he had ever gone without checking email was 40 hours. He even skipped his honeymoon to make sure that he didn't miss any time at work.

The effect of that dedication can be severe. In her book, *For Better Or For Work: A Survival Guide For Entrepreneurs*, Meg Hirshberg describes a business seminar led by her husband Gary Horshberg, Co-founder and CEO of Stonyfield Yogurt:

"As he spoke about the struggle and privation of Stonyfield's early years, the entrepreneurs in the audience redirected their attention to me, sitting among them. Many had tears in their eyes. 'How did you survive as a couple?' they wanted to know. Soon the tales of woe came spilling out. 'My husband left me.' 'My wife divorced me.' 'My mother's not speaking to me.' 'My kids barely know who I am.' 'She's risk-averse; I'm a gambler.' 'He thinks I care more about the company than I do about him. Sometimes I worry that he's right.'"

Those are high prices to pay for setting up your own business and every entrepreneur can relate to them. Putting your business ahead of your family may be natural. It may even be inevitable. But it doesn't come without a cost, and it's not just the entrepreneur who pays.

There are things that you can do to lower the price. Entrepreneurs often leave room for one pressure-releasing activity such as taking a run or going to the gym. Pick an activity that you can do with your partner, and you'll keep one thing that you do regularly together. Set strict limits on your work hours and you can improve productivity and prevent work from expanding to fill the time available. Rand Fishkin improved his work-life balance by seeing a coach who advised him to be home by 7pm and not touch work until the following morning, something he had never done before. He also planned to take a ten-day vacation during which work would be limited to no more than one hour a day... and would be monitored by a timer. Weekends would allow work on just one of the days and also for no more than an hour.

He also learned to say "no" to many of the projects and tasks he might have been willing to accept in the past. That might have been his smartest move. Part of the process of learning to run your own business is understanding the need to delegate, and you can delegate almost every part of your business. What you can't delegate is time with your family.

It also helps to have a partner who is an entrepreneur and who understands the struggle plus can roll their sleeves up and help out. Building something together as a family also provides a way to strike a balance. Listening to family when they tell you to put work aside is also key—because they can help you take a break and be the voice of reason when necessary. Listen to them and don't forget that they need you just as much you need them.

Looking to save two hours a day? Go to www.selfemployed.com/book for twelve tools that I use that allows me to save up to two hours each day so I can spend more time with my family.

7

And Your Family
Supports You Anyway

E
ntrepreneurs might sacrifice time with their family, but they
can't be entrepreneurs with a family if their spouses, parents
and in-laws don't support that sacrifice—at least for a time.
I call this beginning entrepreneurial period the parenthesis period,
or the "bracket" phase. It is somewhat separate, and works better if
you have the support on each end. That support comes in all sorts of
forms but the biggest and the most obvious sign is the signature on
the check.

According to a 2013 report commissioned by Babson and Baruch
Colleges no fewer than 87 percent of new businesses receive early
funding from friends and family. Almost half of backers are peers aged

between 18 and 34, although many of them will be supplying free labor, a place to crash, or a room to run an office rather than money, their contribution saves a young business with no income expenses it can't easily afford.

Even when companies turn to crowdfunding to bring in money, it's usually the people they know best who contribute the first funds and spread the word.

The advantages of tapping friends and family are clear. The median contribution is $15,000 and total funding typically amounts to between $25,000 and $150,000 depending on the depth of the family's pockets. Best of all, it's fast. According to Basil Peters, an exit coach and angel investor, the "family and friends" round is usually completed within a couple of months.

Eight weeks after dreaming up an idea, then turning to the Bank of Mom and Father-in-Law, your business could be up and running, and building its first product.

It looks like an ideal solution. Your family loves you and wants to see you succeed. They trust you and won't make the sort of unreasonable demands that a venture capitalist might make. They're certainly not going to push you into bankruptcy if it all doesn't work out and they don't get their money back. When family members dig into their pockets to support your business idea, they're not making a financial decision in the way the loan officer at the bank will do. And they're not going to tear apart your pitch like a venture capitalist. They're giving you the means to realize your dream, however unlikely that dream might look at the beginning.

But the convenience of taking financial support from friends and family comes with a price. These are people you're going to be spending years with. You're going to be taking their money, and putting it in a high-risk venture. And, because every new business is high-risk—then seeing them every year at Thanksgiving and Christmas, at children's parties and at birthdays, you'll have to (read get to) explain how the company's doing and what you did with their cash.

Take a venture capitalist's money, and if it doesn't work out, you'll never see that person again. Take money from family members to build your business and whether it works or not you will change the relationships within your family.

There are things that you can do to make that change easier. Basil Peters recommends focusing on fairness, alignment and governance. Family members who invest their savings in your business are entitled to a fair share of it and have the right to question the effort you're putting in to turning their investment into a profit. All investors should own the same type of equity, he argues, ideally common shares so that everyone has the same interest in the same result: an increase in the value of the company. And while the first board of governors will usually be made up of the founders who oversee the spending of that friends-and-family money, even at that stage, it's worth remembering that when you try to raise the big bucks, you will need an experienced board of directors.

Of course, the support that a family provides to an entrepreneur isn't just financial. It's also emotional, and once you've got the money out of the way, that support is the most important. It's also only available from family.

It starts with patience. The family of an entrepreneur has to understand that success might come overnight, but it can take years to actually reach that night. Those will be years in which they will hear constantly about the business, about its problems and about its advances. They live with that business just as much as they live with their spouse. So when an entrepreneur receives support from his or her family, it's not just because they want them to succeed. It's because they share their dream. They see the business in exactly the same way and are looking at the exact same vision. They understand that even if they aren't in the office answering emails or designing the packaging, they're still contributing to the building of that dream and can be as proud of that success as the spouse who dreamt it, and make the creation.

The support a family supplies to an entrepreneur continues with listening. Whether a business is large or small, it's lonely at the top. There are things a founder will have on his or her mind that they can't tell a partner or co-founder however close they might be. They can only offload them on a spouse and that spouse needs to lend an open ear. It's not always about giving advice or offering solutions to a problem. The entrepreneur usually knows how to solve a problem. It's about being available to offload a worry, lay the worry to the side and get the entrepreneur up and running again. A best friend can do this, but generally, family does it better.

Perhaps the most important support that an entrepreneur receives from family is the unconditional kind. It's not unusual for a spouse to support a partner as that partner studies their way through medical school or law school but at the end of that process, there should be a high-paying job that will benefit both of them.

For an entrepreneur, the chances of failure are much higher. There is a good chance that the years of long hour, low pay and high stress that would turn someone else into a doctor or Wall Street lawyer could give an entrepreneur nothing but grey hair and boxes of unsold stock. When you have a family that understands the risks and is prepared for failure, there's a great chance that you're an entrepreneur, and a good chance you'll succeed.

8

You Like People
And People Like You

Just about every management book ever written can be summed up with the words: "Great managers don't manage; they lead." They inspire people. They spread their vision throughout their company and they give everyone the sense they're invested in the project. When employees feel that they're as much a part of the company as the entrepreneur who set it up and owns it, that company will succeed.

What makes the difference between an executive who leads and one who has to rely on management? It's not something that you can see. It's not something that you can easily learn, although there are coaches who claim that they can share the techniques. It comes down to something intangible, something you can't measure.

It comes down to charisma. It's all about relationships with people. We both thrive off of other people. Whether it is something I've learned or something they have shared with me that made me laugh or think, I love people, which is what has helped me to become such a successful connector in addition to an entrepreneur. That ability to be a connector and networker has propelled my entrepreneurial success.

An entrepreneur might be a businessperson. They might an engineer, a visionary or an outstanding salesperson. But an entrepreneur is also a "people person." Entrepreneurs have charm. They cajole, inspire, scold, explain and communicate. They have to talk funds out of venture capitalists, deals out of major customers, loans out of bank managers, dedication out of employees, co-operation out of partners and reliability out of suppliers.

The main tool of a software engineer is the keyboard and the screen. A designer makes a living out of a drawing board and a color palette. A writer builds and creates by choosing the right words. The most important tool of an entrepreneur's trade is personal communication: the ability to talk easily with anyone they meet, from a worker on the factory floor to a chairman of the board who once ran a Fortune 500 firm.

The benefits of that communications talent come right at the beginning of the business. Small companies start with a single individual or a small group of friends but as soon as they outgrow the garage, the entrepreneur has to bring in help. For almost half of all businesses, that means turning to the people they know. In *The Founder's Dilemmas: Anticipating and Avoiding the Pitfalls That Can Sink a Startup*, Noam Wasserman, an associate professor of Business Administration at Harvard University, notes that 49 percent of C-level and VP-level hires at startups are drawn from the CEO-founder's personal networks. The more people that you meet, the more people you build a relationship with. And the more people you stay in touch with, the wider your choice of potential partners and employees.

Defining the characteristics that make up charisma isn't easy. In a 2012 interview with *The Economist*, Olivia Fox Cabane, who works as an executive charisma coach for Fortune 500 companies, defines charisma as "a way to get people to like you, trust you and want to do whatever it is that you want them to do. It's what gets people to follow you, or want to work with you, your team, or your company."

In her book, *The Charisma Myth: How Anyone Can Master the Art and Science of Personal Magnetism*, she goes further. Charisma, she argues, can take four distinct forms: focus, visionary, kindness, and authority.

Focus charisma, she says, makes people feel as though they are being listened to and understood. Bill Gates has it and so does Elon Musk. It's what makes a factory worker feel important when the chief executive asks what he does for the company, and listens when the worker tells him how he thinks it could be done better.

We usually see this kind of charisma more often in its absence. We've all met those people at parties who talk with one eye looking over our shoulder in the hope of spotting someone more important. They're not listening and they're not interested in anyone but themselves.

Visionary charisma builds belief. It enables a leader to inspire a disparate group to walk in the same direction and believe in a common cause. Outside the business world, it's the glue that holds together cults and religious followers. For entrepreneurs, it's the difference between another product and a leading product, between customers and evangelists, between users and fanboys. It's what turns a venture capitalist into an investment partner.

Kindness charisma is rarer. Based on warmth and generosity, it makes people feel loved and wanted. It's what's turned the Dalai Lama and Myanmar leader Aung San Suu Kyi into such respected figures. It's more often found in politics where people are encouraged to donate and volunteer time than in business where people are paid and led.

Authority charisma may the most powerful of all, and its origins are in power itself. It's projected through appearance: through clothing and body language, mannerisms and voice. It broadcasts confidence and that self-belief gives confidence to others. This is a form of charisma that should grow naturally with success. The more you achieve, the more confident you feel about your ability to continue to achieve, and the more confident others will feel in your ability to bring them a share of your success. It's not always likeable but it is always unmissable.

None of these forms of charisma comes fully formed. You might start an entrepreneurial career with hints of some of them, enough to begin to pull people around you and to start moving. But as you advance, that natural charisma should spread and deepen. You meet more people, and those people want to know you and stay close to you. They listen when you speak, think about what you say and share your vision with their friends and contacts. Your requests are accepted and persuasion becomes a knock at an open door. The more you succeed in your communications, the more you understand how to communicate effectively. And the more your communications succeed, the more your business succeeds.

Entrepreneurs may start by liking people and they find that the people they meet like them too. But successful entrepreneurs soon discover that like can turn into trust, belief, inspiration and success.

9

Your Imaginary Friend Is Steve Jobs

When you set up your own business, you lose one really enjoyable aspect of working life: you say goodbye to the watercooler. When you're the boss, you don't get to rest an elbow on the top of the bottle and complain about your manager. You don't get to stand around with an office mate and lay out why you think the company should be moving in a completely different direction. Those are privileges that only employees can enjoy.

As the chief executive, you have no peers. You might have a partner but you don't get to make complaints and you can't bask in that warm feeling that comes when you think you know better than anyone else.

You have to take responsibility.

If you think something in the company is wrong, it's up to you to fix it. If you're frustrated at the lack of progress in product development or market penetration, you can't just complain and let off steam; you have to perform a review and build a new plan.

When you're an entrepreneur, it doesn't matter how big the company is or how many employees it might have on its payroll, you're on your own. It doesn't take long at all for an entrepreneur to understand that it really is lonely at the top.

That's one of the reasons that business conferences are so important. Those get-togethers at which entrepreneurs learn about the latest marketing techniques or hear about big data are also opportunities for the owners of businesses to talk to their peers about the challenges of running a company. Entrepreneurs might not be able to hang around the watercooler but we can hang out at the bar at a business conference, and when you go to a business conference you'll find plenty of people doing exactly that.

But, big conferences only take place a few times a year. They're breaks, not part of the work routine. You can find mini-event communities for entrepreneurs, which may take place once a month, or even weekly—but it still means that for the rest of the time an entrepreneur works alone.

Rather, an entrepreneur works with the spirit of another entrepreneur they admire constantly at their side. At one time, that imaginary business friend might have been Jack Welch who increased the value of GE by 4,000 percent during his twenty years at the top. Chief executives running businesses in the eighties and nineties could have done far worse than ask themselves, "What would Jack do?" every time they ran into trouble or wrestled with a difficult decision.

Before the eighties, they might have worked with the ghost of Henry Ford looking over their shoulder or John D. Rockefeller. Every era has had its management heroes, and every entrepreneur has been able to feel inspired by them even if they've never met them or read the biographies so many of them publish after they hang up their ties.

For at least the last decade, that hero has been Steve Jobs. Search on Google for the terms "Steve Jobs" and "entrepreneur" together, and you'll get more than 1.6 million results. Those pages will offer quotes and strategies, case studies and skills. If entrepreneurship had a patron saint, the face of the man in the black turtleneck would already decorate lockets and icons.

There are all sorts of reasons for this dedication to Steve Jobs—reasons that go beyond Apple's position as the world's most valuable company.

Part of it is down to the zeitgeist. Few people could name the head of GE today or even the CEOs of Ford or Chevrolet. Those companies that once dominated American industry have been replaced by technology firms. The tech firms now dominate both in terms of the benefits they bring to the economy and in the effect they have on people's lives.

Everyone knows who set up Facebook and Google, and who now runs Apple. If cars used to be the most important product class in America, it's now mobile phones and the Internet—the area in which Apple operates. Carlos Slim has been the richest man in the world, but because he operates in the field of telecommunications, few people outside his native Mexico have heard of him. Steve Jobs was in the right industry at the right time.

He was also a maverick. Look at pictures of Jack Welch or Steve Forbes, and you'll see a picture of a man in a suit. You'll have to look hard to find a picture of Steve Jobs in a tie. The dress choice is a form of confidence: when you're that good, you don't have to obey the rules.

Most importantly, Steve Jobs was proven to be right even when everyone else said he was wrong. The story of his comeback after he was kicked out of his own company—the one that he himself launched—

and then he led another hugely successful company, then came back and rocketed his first firm to the top of the world—well, it's legendary.

Every entrepreneur will have moments when he or she comes up against resistance. People will tell them that what they want to do can't be done. They'll list all sorts of reasons for their impending failure. They'll be given advice and wonder whether they should take it or whether they should trust their own instincts. Then they'll think of Steve Jobs who always had his own ideas, and who was more right about business than anyone else ever had been before.

There was only ever one Steve Jobs, but every entrepreneur today secretly dreams of being the next one. If you're not just dreaming about creating a world-conquering business but actually building it, and if as you're building it, you might find yourself thinking of how Steve Jobs would make that pitch or manage the design of a product. Your company might not become as big as Apple, but you're an entrepreneur just like him.

10

Your Idea of a Friendly Get-Together is an Hour on Twitter

When you're building your business, you'll find that there's one thing you can't buy, that no one will give you, and that you can't obtain anywhere...time.

Even Warren Buffett only has twenty-four hours in a day, just the same as you. It's what you do with those hours that makes the difference between an entrepreneur and an employee, between success and struggle.

That's why getting together with friends becomes so difficult. It's essential, of course. Those hours away from the office, thinking about something completely different, are vital opportunities to recharge your batteries and rest before taking another leap at your project. It's just difficult to find the hours. Even trying to get a small group together for a drink can take weeks of organizing, especially when you all have families and children who need babysitters, let alone a company that has constant demands.

So when you're leading a life as busy as that of an entrepreneur, it's much easier to relax by spending a bit of time—not with real company— but with your virtual friends on Twitter. Instead of heading to a bar or a restaurant, you flick open a tab or pull out your phone, browse the posts and send a bunch of replies to people you've never met and might never meet. As an entrepreneur you can end up receiving more SMS alerts from people you follow on Twitter than from real friends listed in your address book.

It's not a terrible thing, and many times this action really helps you. For your business, it might even be a good thing. Twitter has much to offer an entrepreneur beyond immediate access to something resembling a social life and the ability to communicate with interesting people without leaving the office.

Some entrepreneurs show how much they identify with their customers. Evgeny Tchebotarev is a co-founder of *500px*, a platform that allows photographers to show off their photos, and even sell licenses to businesses to use their images. But, Evgeny is also a keen photographer himself, and he uses his Twitter account to show off his own photos, which look a lot like the sorts of photos his members upload to his site: a lot of travel images and plenty of artistic landscape imagery. Some of those photos he streams from his Instagram account but the result is a timeline that contains exactly the content you'd expect to see from a keen photographer.

Evgeny rarely uses his timeline for communications. He doesn't talk to customers and he doesn't shoot the breeze with other entrepreneurs. Instead he uses his account for fun mostly, but in the process he puts himself alongside his customers. He shows that he understands their needs because he shares their needs. If his photos are like theirs then the services that his company delivers will be services that people will like and services they will want to use and share.

Other entrepreneurs take different approaches. Tony Hsieh of *Zappos* has a team of people who send out tweets on his behalf. He's turned his official account into a promotional channel that he uses to engage the company's most loyal customers and help to brand a firm that is now a part of the Amazon empire.

Greg Glassman, the founder and CEO of *Crossfit*, also broadcasts messages through his Twitter timeline, mostly related to his views of health and fitness. Some of those views can be strong and controversial. Talking about modern diets, he claims that "The high-carb, low-fat diet was government, university, and industry sponsored malnutrition causal of chronic disease. Your health was sold."

You don't have to agree with him but many people *will* agree with him, and they're likely to be the people who use his company's products. By giving his Twitter stream a strong personality, he gives his followers a strong reason to remain with his firm. But his timeline isn't just broadcasts (and broadsides) about health. He's also happy to engage in conversation and discussions with his followers. Reading his Twitter stream is like watching an ongoing conference about health and fitness.

That's great for Greg Glassman's customers who should find his tweets and conversations interesting to read but it's also great for Greg himself.

When you're passionate about your business—and you *should* be passionate about your business—you want to talk about it all the time. You want to discuss industry issues, talk about what you're doing and vent your frustration at some of the crazy things that happen in your field. (Every field has crazy rules, bureaucracy and dumb ways of doing things.)

The word "dumb," is often offensive to people—however—for entrepreneurs, a short, concise, quick, understandable, direct hit word saves a lot of time. Here, "dumb" encompasses any action that doesn't propel the company forward—such as non-communication, unclear direction, inability to keep employees, ineffectual HR policies, etc.

An entrepreneur needs to talk about this information with someone, but you can't do this with your friends who don't work in your industry—sadly, they won't get it and it merely sounds like you're complaining. Sure, they'll ask you how work is going, in the same way that they'll ask how *you're* doing, but they won't really be interested in your answer. They'd rather talk about how the Mets are doing and about the great restaurant they ate in the previous weekend.

Twitter is one of the few places where you can find people who share your main interest: the topic of your business. You might never meet them. You might not know what they look like. You might not even know where they are. But, you can chat with them all day, exchange messages and at the same time feel a human connection and promote your company. We both love Twitter and use it to share our thoughts and connect with our audiences, peers, and industry.

You don't even have to take time out of your day to do it, but if you do have a quick hour going spare, don't be surprised that as an entrepreneur you find yourself writing short, 140-character posts instead of calling a friend. Most people don't get this obsession, but it's faster—and less messy, as life goes. 140 characters don't leave time for whining. It's direct, straight forward, done.

11

You Thrive in a Group

No entrepreneur ever wants to be an employee. It hurts to take instructions, to think small, to build someone else's vision. But, not everyone who turns their back on a J.O.B. wants to face life as an entrepreneur. The number of C corporations in the United States has shrunk slightly since 1980 but the number of sole proprietorships has almost doubled from around 12 million to around 23 million. Employees are swapping the cubicle for the spare bedroom, setting up home offices and looking for clients. They're becoming freelancers, enjoying their independence while avoiding the responsibility—and the extreme time drag that comes with growing a large business. As long as they have enough satisfying work to fill their schedules, they're content.

Entrepreneurs are different. A business might start in a spare bedroom or a garage but for an entrepreneur, that can only be a humble beginning. Entrepreneurs need to be around people. They need to have smart colleagues to bounce ideas off, voices that challenge them, ideas that inspire them and achievements that compete with them and force them to push themselves to their limits.

Entrepreneurs aren't freelancers. They don't sit at home or in cafes by themselves communicating only through email and Skype chats. For all of the stereotyping about geeks being social misfits with few friends and poor social skills, none of the major tech companies operating today are the result of a single entrepreneur building a company alone. Larry Page and Sergei Brin might not have liked each other much when they first met but like McCartney and Lennon, they needed each other and each brought out the best in the other's work.

However, it's not just inspiration that a group gives to an entrepreneur. Business experts usually describe companies as having three kinds of capital: financial capital; human capital; and social capital.

Financial capital is the funds that allow the company to pay wages, keep the lights on, bring in raw materials and keep the servers running. Human capital is harder to measure but easier to see. It's the skills and talents of the staff that create the company, their ability to write code, design products and come up with effective headlines and sales messages. And social capital is the connections and the shared values that allow a business to leverage co-operation between staff, suppliers and supporters. It's an entrepreneur's force multiplier, the soft power that makes the difference between a country and a superpower. In a business, it may be the most important capital of all.

The benefits of social capital are felt, rather than seen, but the biggest benefit is usually the ability to increase other forms of capital. Entrepreneurs who spend time in groups have connections that are both broad and deep. They know lots of people and the time they've spent with them --those drinks at conference bars, the teambuilding exercises, and the work parties—have built a strong bond with many of them. That means that when an entrepreneur asks if anyone knows a talented coder or a great marketing person, they get replies and recommendations.

Strong social capital delivers stronger human capital.

It does the same for financial capital. Businesses that need funds to get up and running might be able to tap friends and family at first, but at some point, they'll need to be able to get in touch with lenders and investors. The best way to do that is always through introductions. Entrepreneurs need to know people who know the investors and can give them a recommendation. As the *New York Times* put it in its 2013 account of the birth of Twitter: "in Silicon Valley, there is no currency like access. Access to venture capitalists can provide a way for entrepreneurs, like Zuckerberg, to see a company grow by hundreds of thousands of users a day. Access to the tech blogosphere and press can help percolate a fledgling start-up into a multibillion-dollar business."

The newspaper went on to argue that the key to that access is having a narrative, "being an entrepreneur with just the right creation story," like the one that Jack Dorsey had created about his involvement in the founding of the company. But there's more to it than that. The ability to build social capital depends on the way that people see you. It all comes back to the process of knowing you and liking you. The result this time might not be buying from you but it will be an increased willingness to help you.

For an entrepreneur, building that social capital isn't difficult. Some of it can be planned. When you offer advice and help to people who ask for it, you build up credit that you can cash in at a later date. In China, it's called "*guanxi*" and much of the economy depends on it. Social capital builds when you agree to a mentorship, when you stick around after talks at conferences to shoot the breeze and listen to the people you meet. It builds online when people read your blog posts and interact with you on social media. It grows too when you offer public praise for someone who has created a product you admire or when they have delivered a service you value. One entrepreneur knows that the other entrepreneur needs to hear that what they have created has indeed provided value for someone else.

Mostly, this happens naturally. Social capital is born out of the energy you feel when you have a great time with friends. It comes out of that excitement that fills a room at a cocktail party. It's in the laughter that rolls around a table during a dinner with old pals, and you can feel it when someone you like places their hand on your shoulder or gives you a hug before you climb back into your car.

Entrepreneurs might struggle to find the time to meet their friends. They might not be able to get together with groups of peers and acquaintances as often as they like, but being in a group is the time they most come alive. An entrepreneur gathers sustaining energy from a group—the group is a life force. It reminds us that a business isn't about the bottom line; it's about people and the effect that a good business has on people's lives.

12

You Pick Your Crowd with Care

When getting together with friends is both difficult and valuable, entrepreneurs have to choose their crowds carefully. For most people the only criteria used when forming friendships is shared humor and shared values. We like to be around people who make us laugh and who make us feel comfortable.

What happens when we meet people who aren't like us? Do factory workers make friends easily with managers? Do retail workers invite doctors and law professors to share the barbeque and chat over a cold beer? Do we pick crowds made up of lots of different kinds of people, with different backgrounds, jobs and outlooks?

In general, we don't. Sociologists have consistently found that people who are similar in terms of income, politics and level of education tend to flock together. We might be tolerant and open to everyone but on the whole, we make friends with people who are like us.

For an entrepreneur, that's a problem because entrepreneurs are upwardly mobile. They work hard to increase their income, and in the process they might increase their education and even switch their politics. They change, and sometimes they don't even notice that. As they move up they leave friends and acquaintances behind, and in the process, they show them what they could be if they shared their drive and their determination to succeed. Entrepreneurs, much as they may wish to, don't stay static. It's impossible.

Those friends then, have three choices: they can accept those differences and focus on the similarities that remain (success doesn't change people entirely), while encouraging their entrepreneurial friend to keep growing; they can feel inspired by their success and join them on their journey; or they can reach up and try to drag their high-flying friend back down, making themselves feel better at their own lack of movement by restricting the flight of others.

That last choice happens far too often. Every entrepreneur has felt it. We've all sat in a bar with a friend, laid out a plan and listened to a thousand reasons why it's a terrible idea and why even if it is a good idea, we're not the right person to make it happen. I call this, "momentum drag." It's like an awful headwind in an airplane.

Those are difficult moments. It's hard to build a business. It's challenging to raise the cash, find the staff, develop the products and bring in clients and customers. It's hardest of all to manage our own doubts.

All entrepreneurs have doubts. They all have moments when pitches are met with silence, products fail, and customers and employees walk away leaving them wondering how to move forward. At those times, even the most dedicated of entrepreneurs can start to believe they might be better off saying that they tried, dusting off their résumés, and looking for a safer way to pay the mortgage. Those dark moments are made even darker by friends pulling them off their path; bashing them personally, or bashing their ideas. Truth is great—bashing is not.

That's why entrepreneurs have to be careful about their crowds, and they have to be willing to change them. Over time, the people I keep close have changed as I have evolved as an entrepreneur and person. It's a natural progression for everyone but especially important if you are an entrepreneur because you need to keep moving forward and don't want others around that don't have the same passion, work ethic, or energy.

It's a process that should happen naturally. A mechanic who wants to open his own auto repair shop will initially hang around with the guys who passed him the spanner as he lay under the Mustang. As he starts to hire mechanics though, his old friends will start to look at him in the same way that they see their own bosses. Either they'll move on in their own directions, opening their own repair shops or taking more responsible roles at racetracks or other businesses, or the relationship risks breaking down.

At the same time, the garage owner will be spending more time with other entrepreneurs. Issues that might not have concerned him before, such as parking regulations, crime rates and local business taxes will have him sitting in meetings with other local business owners. He might start attending meetings at the local chamber of commerce and take seminars to improve his marketing and recruitment techniques. As he meets more local business owners, they introduce him to other business owners. As he becomes less of a mechanic and more of a manager, his mind expands and his social circle changes.

For some old acquaintances, that process can be accelerated. Just as some of an entrepreneur's old contacts will try to make themselves feel better by pulling their go-getting friend down so others will try to pull themselves up on their friend's back. Tell someone that business is going great, that you're expanding the office and sales are doing better than expected, and eventually one of your old friends will pull you aside and ask you for a loan. Or they'll pitch an idea to you and feel offended when you tell them to run with it instead of making them a partner and making it happen yourself.

Or worse, they'll ask for a job and you'll be faced with employing a friend or explaining why, despite your booming business, they just don't have any skills that you can use.

None of those relationships or conversations will make you comfortable. None of them will help you through the doubts and the difficulties of being an entrepreneur that other entrepreneurs can help you with.

Entrepreneurs can keep members of their old crowd, but they rarely keep all of the members of their old crowd. They stay in touch with the people who truly respect them, understand them and wish them the best. The rest they replace. They have to.

13

Some People Think You're Nuts

The headline said it all. "The Mad Billionaire Behind GoPro: The World's Hottest Camera Company," was how *Forbes* pitched its 2013 profile of Nick Woodman, the then-37-year old founder of the camera firm that let extreme sports enthusiasts broadcast their antics:

> Already hopped up on Red Bull, tempered by a liter of coconut water, Woodman darts about the cabin, occasionally breaking conversation to unleash his trademark excited wail that friends liken to a foghorn: "YEEEEEEEEEEEEEOW." A flight attendant emerges with breakfast on a silver platter. "You know what the best thing about morning ski trips are?" he asks the

cabin rhetorically. "McDonald's!" And with that he inhales a McGriddle in all of three bites.

What *Forbes* calls a "man-teen routine" isn't the only thing that's crazy about Nick Woodman. Ten years earlier, having seen his online gaming company go belly-up in the dotcom crash, he had returned from a five-month surfing trip to Australia and Indonesia with the germ of an idea. Normal life stopped. He locked himself in his bedroom, put on a Camelback filled with diluted Gatorade, and put in eighteen-hour workdays with a drill and his mother's sewing machine to create a prototype for a new kind of camera. He didn't even take bathroom breaks; his bedroom had a sliding door that opened onto some bushes.

The idea might have been crazy. The way he made it happen might have been even crazier. But it also worked. The year before *Forbes'* profile, GoPro had grossed more than half a billion dollars in revenues.

Entrepreneurs are often thought of as nuts. They should be, and not just because of the new business failure rates that every entrepreneur is aware of and does it anyway. It's because there are only two kinds of business ideas.

The first are ideas for products and services that are completely new. When Apple brought out the iPad, no one knew if it was going to work. There was nothing like it on the market, previous small attempts had failed and little sign that there would be a demand for a plus-sized iPod Touch. It was easy then for critics to say that the idea was ridiculous, and if you look back on the Web, you can find plenty of articles with headlines like this 2009 story in *InfoWorld*: "Why Apple's Rumored iTablet Will Fail Big Time." You could have made the world's biggest omelet with all the egg tech writers had on their faces the following year.

Plenty of other products from pet rocks to plastic wishbones, and yes to the iPhone fart apps (you're welcome!) —might have seemed nuts when they were made but went on to make small fortunes for their creators. The ability to write text messages that anyone can see sounds nuts until you lose half an hour browsing tweets. That people would want to send each other pictures that disappear as soon as they're seen sounds insane until you remember how much Snapchat is worth.

Plan to do something new, something original, something that no one else has done before and people will always tell you that you're crazy.

And, they may be right. If no one has ever created a product like the one you want to make, there are only two possible reasons: it's a terrible idea and everyone else can see it; or it's a genius idea that only you have seen.

You won't know which it is until you've made the product available to the public.

Truly original products are rare. Few products come out of nowhere. Even Facebook had plenty of predecessors in the form of MySpace and Harvard's Freshman Yearbook. Most product development takes the form of an improvement on something that people are already using. Entrepreneurs often look for a weakness in a product they otherwise love and either fill the niche or try to compete with a better version, or a cheaper version. The iPad didn't have the tablet computer market to itself for long. While it remains the most advanced tablet, it is also the most expensive and other manufacturers have filled the market with cheaper, lower tech versions.

When the idea for your business isn't a completely original idea but an improvement on an existing one, people still think you're nuts. They think you're nuts not because the idea is bad but because they don't see how you will be able to compete with the much bigger companies that already dominate the market. You're starting way behind, (they think). They already have a connection with customers. You have to persuade customers to give up something they like for something they don't know they like.

You have to be crazy to do something like that.

Some people will always think that entrepreneurs are a bit nuts. They have to be nuts to be the first to bring something new to the market, and they have to be nuts to be the second, third or fourth to bring something to the market.

They have to be nuts to put in the hours they work with such a low chance of success. And they have to be nuts to take the risks that they take.

Yet, entrepreneurs don't think they're nuts. They're believe they're driven—but they understand that leaving a great business idea unrealized *really would* drive them nuts.

14

Your Life Partner Totally Gets You

For a long time, the pinned tweet at the top of Brianna Wu's timeline showed a video of the Super Mario Maker level that she created for her husband, Frank. We hear him whooping in pleasure as he makes Mario jump on mushrooms, then we laugh at his frustration when, fifteen seconds into the video, Mario runs straight into a wall that Brianna has made with a gap too small for the character to bounce through.

It's clear that the couple don't just have the kind of close relationship that allows them to tease each other publicly; they also have the same interests. Both are happy to spend time playing computer games and both share the same sense of humor.

However, it's not easy being the partner of Brianna Wu. She's an entrepreneur, the co-founder and Head of Development at Giant Spacekat, an iOS gaming company. As a speaker on women in tech, she has also become a lightning rod for Gamergate campaigners—male computer game players who have a problem with women in the video game industry.

In addition to the usual long hours and worries about financial stability faced by every spouse of an entrepreneur, Frank Wu also has to support his wife through the very real death threats and hacking attacks that she receives from her opponents. The couple have seen their personal details and private lives splashed across gamer forums, and following the advice of the police and the FBI, have even been forced to flee their home.

If it's always hard to be the life partner of an entrepreneur, it's far, far harder when that entrepreneur has to battle vilification online at the same time as building a business. But Frank Wu shares his partner's enthusiasm for her business and for the industry in which she works. He's listed as a co-founder of the company. The couple are sometimes interviewed together, and as a Hugo-award-winning science fiction artist, they also share a love of science fiction and space.

That's often how entrepreneurs work. They choose spouses who understand their business and its needs as deeply as they understand their spouse's personality.

Those are very different needs. All life partners give each other emotional support; it comes with the ring, I suppose. They may also provide financial support. Even when fewer women worked, it wasn't unusual for wives to support their husbands through medical or law school before the positions reversed once the husband started his career.

But, the life partner of an entrepreneur needs to go even further. When an employee returns home from the office and releases his or her frustration with their workplace, it often comes down to office politics, the chances of receiving a promotion or a complaint about a manager who doesn't understand them. Those are people problems. Everyone experiences them, and anyone can offer advice about how to deal with them. Often, the life partner has to do little more than listen and provide a space for their partner to vent.

The issue is that entrepreneurs also bring very specific problems home. They worry about funding rounds and development challenges. They struggle with business partners and have to battle suppliers who deliver late or not at all. They have to field complaints and motivate the same employees who are now at home venting to *their* life partners.

Because they're at the top of the company, entrepreneurs rarely have someone to discuss these issues with at work. When they return home, often late, they turn to the person they know best—not just for support but also for practical advice. They want to know which offer of funding they should take. They want to know which growth strategy is likely to be the most effective. They want to know whether they should fire their talented CTO or continue to put up with his resistance to their instructions.

Entrepreneurs have to make decisions. Those decisions are often difficult, and they don't always have someone in the office who can give them advice.

Not all entrepreneurs choose life partners who also want to run their own businesses or who even work in the same industry. Increasingly, people are choosing life partners with a similar education, similar outlooks, and similar backgrounds. That means that when an entrepreneur comes home and starts discussing some amazing growth hack technique that they heard about that day, there's a good chance that their life partner will know exactly what they mean. They're also likely to be equally enthusiastic about the idea, and be full of their own suggestions about the best way to implement them.

In my own life, I've been very fortunate to have found a partner who shares an entrepreneurial spirit as well as the same passion and sense of humor where we know when it's time to work and when we can take things a little less seriously. It's a journey and she is fully vested in taking the same path to see where it will take us along with our latest addition to the family. Whether you are an entrepreneur or not, you have to make the most out of the life we are given so find someone that has that perspective. It will be tough and challenging, but it will be fun and memorable, too.

Life partners of entrepreneurs set themselves up for a very special way of living. The company will come first. Money will be short, at least initially. Hours will be long and home is never more than the office's more comfortable annex. Office people may call at a moments notice, just drop in for a little help on a project—you know—open office hours day or night? But an entrepreneurs partner totally gets it, and no entrepreneur could ever succeed without the understanding and support that they receive from their life partner.

Part 3

Personality

There is no one entrepreneurial personality. Entrepreneurs have personalities that range from outgoing and attention-seeking to introverted and shy, from unpredictable and emotional to cool and rational. When we can use the term "entrepreneur" to describe both someone as modest as Warren Buffett and as showy and out there as Donald Trump, it's clear that personality itself is no definer of the ability to build a business.

Entrepreneurs do have personality traits. They might not have all of those traits but they will have many of them and even those they don't appear to have will often lie there hidden or partly-hidden, only revealing themselves when they're in the boardroom, pitching to an investor or wondering how to outflank a competitor and close a deal.

Charisma is a part of those traits. Entrepreneurs have to persuade and inspire. They have to bring employees, investors, partners, and customers with them on their journey.

They know the difference between obeying the law and breaking the rules, between being opinionated and winning an argument, and between obstinacy and flexibility. (Also, I'll just say it—an entrepreneur knows how to be obstinate while appearing flexible.) This is a good quality in that, anyone can say anything ensconced in offensive language or phrasing that gets them in trouble—but the ability to still pull out the win with a winning way is important for anyone—but especially important for an entrepreneur.

They have confidence that (hopefully) stops them short of an arrogance that drives them into fatal mistakes. They're rebellious and creative, practical and grounded. They know how to dream but they also know how to turn those dreams into a plan, and how to communicate that plan so that others are as enthusiastic as they are about making that plan real.

Entrepreneurs are all of these things and they're driven and passionate plus they get things done.

15

You Have Charisma

Walk into Warren Buffett's small office in Omaha, Nebraska, and you'll find a lot of things that might surprise you. The desk is old; it used to belong to his father. There's no computer terminal on it; despite his friendship with Bill Gates, the only thing that Buffett knows how to do with a computer is play Bridge. And he doesn't have his degrees from the University of Nebraska-Lincoln or Columbia Business School splattered all over his walls. Instead, just down the corridor from his presidential "Medal of Freedom" hangs a frame on the wall containing a certificate that shows that "Warren E. Buffet has successfully completed the Dale Carnegie Course in Effective Speaking, Leadership, Training, and the Art of Winning Friends and Influencing People." (Surprised? I was.)

Buffett, who completed the course in January 1952, says that it changed his life. It's enabled him to stand in front of an audience, deliver talks and make presentations. It's helped him to turn the world's most successful investment company into an educational institution as well as a profitable firm, and it's turned him from a successful investor into the Sage of Omaha.

Dale Carnegie gave Warren Buffett what every successful entrepreneur needs and few investors possess: *charisma*.

It's a quality that sounds magical, and its effects certainly look like magic. Audiences, even skeptical ones, listen. They absorb what they're being told, pay attention to the information they receive and they act on it. They buy or invest. They tell their friends about the company and they value their relationship to the entrepreneur. Charisma is what makes the difference between a leader with a following and someone taking a walk alone. It's what turns someone with an idea into an entrepreneur with a growing business.

Some people have it naturally. If you've ever been to a party and seen a group of people standing in the corner where one person is holding court, you'll have seen the effect of natural charisma. When that individual moves to another part of the house, the party drifts with them. It's effortless and even unconscious, and sometimes it's temporary but for as long as the person manages to hold into it, it looks remarkable.

However, that natural charisma is rare. Many of the world's biggest entrepreneurs are likely to have started with some degree of charisma but many will have also taken lessons to learn how to develop it, strengthen it and hold onto it. Once, like Warren Buffett, they would have turned to Dale Carnegie, but there's no shortage of coaches who can help entrepreneurs charm investors, wow customers and impress reporters.

Regardless of who's doing the teaching, the principles of developing and strengthening charisma have barely changed since the days of Dale

Carnegie. There's no secret formula and nothing complex about the ability to persuade people to listen to you and like you. Carnegie himself breaks making people like you into six simple lessons.

Whether it is in person or an emoji, smiling helps. Everyone hopes that the people they meet enjoy their company and a broad smile delivered right at the moment you meet puts people at their ease, and makes them feel that they're in good company.

You should also remember another persons' name. That's harder, but Dale Carnegie reminds his students that a person's name is to that person "the sweetest and most important sound in any language." Again, some people seem to have photographic memories. They can recall the names of everyone they meet, together with their birth dates, pet names and favorite colors. But if you're surprised that a business leader that you met once, years ago, can remember your name, don't put it down to natural charisma. It's more likely to be the result of a learned mnemonic strategy that allows them to permanently match a name to a face. *If they can learn how to do it, so can you.*

The other four strategies that Dale Carnegie recommends all come down to the same thing. He recommends being a good listener as you encourage people to talk about themselves. He suggests that you talk about the things that they find interesting, and that as they talk, you make them feel important. And he says that you should be genuinely interested in other people.

That's the crucial one. That's the core of charisma that makes all the difference.

Charisma is never about what someone sees in the person who possesses it. It's how they see themselves in the person who possesses it. When you're as curious about people as you are about your business, all the rest should follow. You'll want to ask them questions. You'll want to listen to them when they answer. You'll smile at that reply and you'll remember their name because they're telling you something unique.

And, what you learn when you listen to them will be valuable. It tells you who people are and what they think. It reminds you that products and success are ultimately about people and the effect the services you create have on those people. It makes people believe that you have charisma, and it shows that you're an entrepreneur.

16

You Believe Everyone Has Laws—
And Everyone Else Has Rules

It's hard to read a book about entrepreneurs, business-building or management without being told to look at what Steve Jobs did, and do it like that. One person says otherwise, and he should know. Richard Branson has been no less successful than Steve Jobs has been and in a wider range of businesses. In a 2014 interview with *Inc.* magazine Branson pointed out all of the ways in which Steve Jobs broke the rules of good management that he had previously outlined.

Jobs micromanaged and failed to delegate, was brusque with people and was more likely to insult them than motivate them. "Somehow it worked. Sometimes my rules are meant to be broken," Branson said.

"[But] personally, I think his approach for the vast majority of people running companies will not work."

That Steve Jobs broke the rules shouldn't come as too large a surprise to anyone, and it's not as though an entrepreneur who started with a record store and ended up owning a rail company, an airline and even a space tourism business can talk about staying on the straight and narrow. Entrepreneurs rarely get anywhere unless they break the rules.

Before you can break the rules, you have to know the rules. You need to know what other leaders have done, what the standard route from A to B would look like and how to follow it.

Then you can question it, and that's where the magic starts to happen. That's when you start to forge your own path, a road that has few competitors and that can take you where you want to go faster and more efficiently than anyone else.

Joanne Wilson, a serial investor and co-founder of the Women's Entrepreneur Festival, once described on her blog at GothamGal.com, a board meeting at a non-profit she chaired. "[We] were discussing how we were going to undertake a particular project. One board member, who had been in the non-profit world for years said, 'you can't do it that way because that is not how they do it in the non-profit world.' Needless to say, I replied that we were not going to do it the way you are supposed to do it, but the way we think we should. In the end, our way was hugely successful and that NY organization is now a global organization."

That account describes both how rules are made, and how they're broken. People who have been in an industry for a long time become used to doing things a certain way. They build products that look a lot like products that have sold well in the past. They market those products through the same channels that their competitors use with similar messages and to audiences that other companies before them have already identified. They do what they see has worked and they assume that the reason that no one does it any differently is that different doesn't work. If they have a system that's already functioning, why take the risk with a new system that might fail?

Yet, that's not what the entrepreneur who started the company did. The founders of Whole Foods Market were the owners of two small health food stores in Austin, Texas who wondered why stores that sold organic and healthy food always had to be tiny. Why couldn't they be the size of traditional supermarkets? They questioned the traditional way of doing things, and came up with something completely new. They made their own market.

When Michael Dell started his computer company in his dorm at the University of Texas in Austin, he didn't sell complete machines as other computer outlets were doing. He let buyers order the parts they wanted so that they could receive a custom-built unit. The overheads were lower and customers were happier.

A new entrepreneur setting up a new business will always struggle to compete against more powerful competitors doing the same thing unless they have something new to offer. If they aren't prepared to change the rules, they can't be ready to change the status quo.

Often, the source of those new ideas is experience brought from somewhere else.

Joanne Wilson's knowledge of the commercial world meant that she brought a new vision to the non-profit sector. But sometimes it's just an insight, a willingness to question and the courage to take a risk that other people were afraid to take, like a chef who wonders what happens if you use orange instead of lemon or a telesales worker who notices that customers tend to be people putting down roots and pitches to names on marriage and mortgage lists instead of the list the company supplies. (Michael Dell did that when he was a high school student; he earned more than his teacher that year.)

It helps too when an entrepreneur has little to lose. PC's Limited, the precursor to Dell Inc., cost just $1,000 to set up and Michael Dell was just 27 when his company made the Fortune 500 list. If he had failed, his losses would have been small and he would have had plenty of time to bounce back and try again.

Put together an entrepreneurial spirit, courage and an idea, and you'll have the beginnings of a new business venture.

However, there's a limit. Rules describe how businesses operate. No one writes them; they develop by themselves like a track that many people have walked down. Laws, though, *are* written, and they're written to protect people from harm. They ensure that all businesses compete in a fair environment and that customers can buy with confidence.

Only criminals break laws; successful entrepreneurs spot opportunities and break the rules.

17

You Know Your Limits

Before you can begin building a business, you need a certain amount of capital. You need an idea, a product, a website probably. You need a lot of things to create a company, but there's one thing you need more than anything else: you need knowledge.

You need to know the market. You need to know how to create the product, you need to know who is likely to buy it and you need to know how you can put it in their hands.

There's one piece of knowledge you need to know more than any other: you need to know yourself. It's the most important piece of information anyone can acquire, and for an entrepreneur it's essential. You need to know what you can do. You need to know where you excel. And you need to know your weaknesses.

That's not knowledge that you can find in any books. None of the webinars and business conferences or information products you might buy will contain a roadmap to your personality. Some of them might explain how you can assess yourself but it will still be up to you to conduct that assessment and understand the results.

And, it will be up to you to act on those results.

This may be the biggest challenge that any entrepreneur faces. In fact, it's probably the biggest challenge that *anyone* faces but for an entrepreneur, the stakes are so much higher. Someone who fails to understand themselves, can harm their relationships with an angry word or find themselves repeating unproductive work patterns through constant procrastination or complaining, but they muddle through. These people can apologize, fix the damage, and repair their reputation. They might not reach stellar heights of success but they can still make do and move ahead.

When an entrepreneur fails to know themselves, the business stalls. The entrepreneur's initial drive and momentum and determination are enough to get the idea out of the garage, into an office and onto shelves but at some point their weaknesses block their progress. When a business struggles to grow, it soon starts to shrink. Competitors shoot past, frustration replaces momentum and as good staff starts to leave for more successful companies what they leave behind is a much weaker version of what the business should have been.

Understanding our limits requires overcoming a host of different biases that psychologists say we all use unconsciously to order our world and make sense of our experience. For both of us, as entrepreneurs, we have done a significant amount of soul searching, reflection, and analysis as well as sought feedback from others to understand our limitations and then figure out how to change them.

Hindsight bias, for example, makes events that surprised us when they happened expected or even inevitable. How many times have you told yourself, long after an event, that you knew it was going to happen? Clearly, you *didn't* know it was going to happen because if you had, you would have done something about it. You would have either prevented it or taken action that would have allowed you to profit from it.

When you say you *did know*, take a second to think what that actually means. Did you *feel* something in those moments before to which you *should* have paid attention? Did you have a "gut" feeling you didn't follow? Think deeply about this. As an entrepreneur you have to pay attention to your instincts—especially if they are usually correct.

Next time you have an idea cross your mind that you should *maybe consider*—well, take an extra few minutes and—*maybe consider it*! Don't shove the thought out of your mind. Bring it out of your mind and onto to table and make an informed decision. If, in the end, you are right, you will trust yourself better. And, if in the end, you were wrong, you will also trust yourself better, because you heard your own inner thoughts and considered them.

Hindsight bias, though, is a valuable technique because it makes the world more predictable and less frightening. It makes us feel in control. But it also allows us to oversimplify situations and prevents us from seeing the real origins of an event. *It stops us from learning.* If a product launch fails, it's not enough to say shrug and say, "Well, I expected that." We have to understand *why* the launch failed and *where* that failure became baked in so that we can avoid those mistakes in the future.

Impact bias relates to that future. It fails to predict how we'll feel when an event we've planned actually occurs because we can never imagine all of the complexities that that event will include. You might dream of your product selling millions and you might imagine the joy you'll feel, but when that success doesn't happen suddenly, like the winning of a lottery, but slowly with data-driven decisions putting up sales gradually month after month, the impact can be smaller than you might expect.

That brings a danger of disappointment even at the moment of your greatest success.

The most dangerous form of bias for an entrepreneur though is *confirmation bias*. Nobel prize-winning psychologist Daniel Kahneman has described it as a technique that allows the brain to think fast. It's why we choose to pay more attention to the arguments that support a position we've already taken than evidence that proves we're wrong. If you've ever had a political argument with someone, you'll have seen that bias in action. It doesn't matter how much data you pull out or how much evidence, the person you're talking to will skip right past the facts and focus on what they believe to be true.

There are ways around all of these biases. Researchers have found that one way of overcoming confirmation bias is to print the arguments in small type or in a font that's hard to read. The extra effort forces the reader to think about what they're reading instead of scanning and focusing on the parts that they agree with.

The challenge for entrepreneurs isn't to acknowledge that they have limits. We all do. It's to recognize those limits, to understand our weaknesses, and to overcome them. There's a very easy way to do that: we hire people whose strengths complement our failings.

All entrepreneurs start with a certain amount of knowledge. Successful entrepreneurs come to know where they fall short and find great people who can fill those gaps. They also are on a continual learning curve themselves for knowledge of *anything* business.

18

You Have Opinions and You're Not Afraid To State Them

I t takes courage to be an entrepreneur. Not the same sort of courage that has firefighters racing up burning buildings or Marines landing on beaches. But it is the courage to take risks with money and time and effort that could so easily be avoided. It would be so much easier to look for a job and take instructions. Someone else would take responsibility and all you'd have to do is fill the hours and collect the pay check. There would be no tough decisions and the years to retirement would be mostly clear. Even if you lose that job—and there's little job security these days—you could just go out and get another one.

But, entrepreneurs aren't built for a life like that. *"It would be so much easier to look for a job and take instructions."* (As stated above.)

NO! It's *not* easier for an entrepreneur to do that, and it just plain doesn't work. An entrepreneur enjoys taking risks. They get a kick out of taking control. And, they're confident enough to believe that it will all work out. Entrepreneurs don't care what people think. They can't because if they did care they would have to listen to all of those people telling them that their plan won't work and that they have no business starting a new business.

At the core of every entrepreneur is a spine of steel and an unshakeable belief that they're right. Now, diminished mental capacity people are sometimes the most stubborn people on the planet, so you have to know which one you are.

We both realize that we are strong-willed people and it's helped us as entrepreneurs to continue to push through barriers we've experienced along the way. I've personally had people tell me that a business idea wasn't going to fly, and I told them—and proved—otherwise. Stating my opinion that it would work was impetus for me to work that much harder to make it a reality.

In business, this is an essential component. But it has a habit of leaking into areas outside the office. Look through the some of the bizarre things that Elon Musk has said, for example, and you're going to see opinions that range from the visionary and the clever to the insane and the dangerous. He's predicted that driving cars will, one, become illegal: "It's too dangerous. You can't have a person driving a two-ton death machine." He's recommended a hyperloop as the only option for super-fast travel short of real teleportation. Yet, he's also said that if Tesla published patents, the Chinese would use them as "recipe books," and he's suggested dropping thermonuclear bombs on the poles of Mars to warm the planet and make it habitable. Okay, Musk makes big brash statements. Most entrepreneurs do this.

Musk is certainly not someone who's afraid to take risks, even in the riskiest field of space travel, and he's also not afraid to state his opinion, no matter how crazy that opinion might sound.

As long as Musk's companies are growing and succeeding, those strange opinions aren't a problem. They can actually be an asset. When Musk started musing about building a hyperloop in California that would whisk people between Los Angeles and San Francisco in little more than half an hour, there were two reactions. One was from people who thought he must be crazy: it would cost a fortune; it wouldn't work; at more than 700 mph, the speeds would be too dangerous.

The other reaction was to look at the achievements of someone who had built a multi-billion dollar online payment system, put a fast, affordable and beautiful all-electric car on the road, and was sending rockets into space, and bringing them back to land upright on landing pads in the middle of the sea, and wonder whether he should be taken seriously.

Because those opinions are coming from someone who has already made big ideas happen, they're different to ideas thrown around among friends in a bar. Anyone can talk about the benefits of flying cars or the advantages of a space elevator over rockets but when you're an entrepreneur, those opinions have a greater weight. They're not just thoughts spoken aloud; they could be the first stage in a plan that might actually go somewhere.

It doesn't matter how bizarre your opinion is, if you have a record of success some people will want to dismiss it and even laugh at it, but others will start to wonder whether you couldn't actually make it happen. They'll take your opinion seriously. (In January 2016, Hyperloop Technologies announced the start of construction of a test track at 50-acre facility in North Las Vegas. The company even released footage of the tubes.)

The problem is what happens before you reach that success. It's one thing for Elon Musk to talk about hyperloops after making an electric car and a reusable rocket. It's another for a new entrepreneur to talk about personal transport drones while they're still building their online printing platform. Or even while they're still an employee. Start telling people at work that the product you're making will be made redundant by your vision of the future and that the CEO hasn't got a clue about the direction the company needs to take, and you're not likely to last too long in that job.

A lack of obvious success won't stop an entrepreneur from sharing their opinion though. It just means that fewer people will take it seriously, at least until that platform is worth billions and those drones start operating test routes from the suburbs to the inner cities.

Entrepreneurs aren't like other people. Everyone has ideas and everyone has opinions. But most people don't act on those ideas. Entrepreneurs *do* act on their ideas and they shape the opinions that other people will later claim as their own. Entrepreneurs aren't just willing to state their opinions, they're willing to absorb the ridicule those opinions might receive when they first state them, and they're willing to take the risk in making their ideas happen.

19

You Change Your Mind as Often as The World Changes Its

I n July 2015, Steve Huffman, co-founder of Reddit and the company's new chief executive, announced that he would be shutting down threads and communities that focused on what he called "reprehensible" topics. "Neither Alexis [Ohanian, another Reddit cofounder] nor I created Reddit to be a bastion of free speech, but rather as a place where open and honest discussion can happen," he wrote on the site's announcement page.

It didn't take long for Reddit's users to find a 2012 interview with *Forbes* in which Alexis Ohanian had described the site as "a bastion of free speech on the worldwide web."

That's embarrassing. It's never comfortable when someone calls out and can show that you're saying the exact opposite of what you said in the past. But for an entrepreneur, that flexibility is essential.

All entrepreneurs have strong opinions. They know their minds and once they decide to take action, they have to believe whole-heartedly in the course they've chosen, or at least *show* that they believe whole-heartedly in the course they've chosen because everyone has doubts. Everyone has moments when they wonder whether they've made the right decision or whether they should have taken a different path some time ago. Those doubts are what come before the reviews and the meetings and the decision to try something else. But until that decision has been taken, those doubts have to be kept hidden.

The alternative is for those doubts to be proven to be true.

When employees see that the CEO is thinking twice about a product or a marketing plan, they invest less. They cut their hours, work slower, fail to check for bugs or mistakes. What's the point in putting their all into a project if that project is about to be cancelled? Nothing creates that end-of-term feeling like the sense that something is about to come to an end.

Investors and customers react in the same way. No investor is going to put money into a company unless they believe that the chief executive is completely committed to the course the company is taking. And no customer will buy a product if they think that product is about to be discontinued, and take with it the support, parts, and the sense that they've bought something worth owning.

When an entrepreneur changes direction, that change will always comes suddenly. They pivot quickly and it's obvious. This scares some people, especially the person who does not understand business workings. Because so many if not most companies believe they have to hide their workings, we only see a company facing in one direction one day then a completely different direction the next. These companies believe that no one notices—and some people don't. But, when Microsoft released Windows 8, it continued to state that the operating system had no need for a start menu—right up until the moment it announced an update that included a return to the start menu. At the time, the *Financial Times* called the move the "most prominent admission of failure for a new mass-market consumer product since Coca-Cola's New Coke fiasco."

That's a harsh line to take, especially when the Microsoft decision wasn't a failure in the end, but a needed daring pivot to what it knew was the best option for the company. And, the alternative would have been to continue with a design and functionality its customers had shown they didn't like. Microsoft should have been hailed as using "brilliant" deductions of deciphering what it was their audience wanted, needed and asked for. Microsoft could clearly see that fewer people would have upgraded. More and more people would have turned to alternatives like Macs and Chromebooks and Microsoft would have lost market share and revenues and would have taken a heavy blow to its most important product.

That's the difference between entrepreneurs and everyone else. Microsoft was merely acting somewhat like an entrepreneur.

The usual scenario in life is to present someone with evidence that their opinion is wrong and they shrug it off. We all do it. It's part of confirmation bias. We ignore facts that show we're on the wrong path and we jump on any small suggestion that proves that we're right.

For the most part, it doesn't matter. If your opinion about global warming or gun laws is wrong, it's only going to affect one vote. It's not really going to affect the country; there are plenty of other people who can offset your opinion. Because there are no real consequences to being wrong—and plenty of *personal* consequences to admitting that you *were* wrong—people who aren't entrepreneurs can happily *stay* wrong.

When evidence starts to mount that an entrepreneur's opinion about the market for a product was off, there *are* consequences. If they stick to their guns, dig in their feet, or remain in a shocked stupor—the entire firm could crash. Money will certainly continue to be lost. So, regardless of the confidence with which they once talked about their plans and their products, entrepreneurs have to change direction and indeed change their minds when their customers ask for the change. When the facts change, their opinion has to change too, at least as far as those opinions affect the business. In business, being wrong carries a high price.

Changes happen all the time, and they have to. No business ever grows without testing. No product ever reaches the market in the version that first appeared in the mind of the company's founder. In fact, there's often very little relationship between a founder's vision and the product that rolls off the production line, and even less of a relationship to later versions of the product that rolls off the production line.

When Steve Huffman announced that free speech on Reddit had its limits, he was doing his best to save a platform that had become a byword for trolling and misogyny. He and his fellow co-founders had believed that if they allowed people to say what they wanted, *common decency* would stop them from saying reprehensible things. Showing that he was wrong wouldn't have been easy but once it became clear that he *was* wrong watching Reddit die would have been harder still.

Entrepreneurs might have strong opinions but they're also strong enough to change them.

20

You Believe In Yourself

magine that your manager calls you into their office and informs you that from now on you will have to work longer hours, perhaps as many as twelve a day. Plus, weekends. Your pay would be cut. She couldn't say by how much or for how long but it's possible that you wouldn't receive any pay at all for several months. You will also have to pay for the desk and the chair and the computer, and even the coffee. On the other hand, there's a chance—a small chance—that you might make a lot of money in a couple of years.

Faced with that prospect, there's a good chance that you'd dust off your résumé and start looking for a workplace that treats you better.

This scenario is exactly what entrepreneurs picture in their minds, live through, and forge a path into this place every time they quit their jobs and start a business of their own. They make this change and live in these conditions because they want their independence, but they also do it because they believe that the sacrifices they make in the short term will pay them back over the long term. They believe that they will make a lot of money in a couple of years or so, enough to overcome those lost earnings at the beginning. The entrepreneur has seen others make a go of it and find success, and they feel that they will succeed as well.

Entrepreneurs know that most small businesses fail, as said before. They know that their chances of success are small. But they also believe in themselves enough to believe that they will be the exception. The entrepreneurs believe they will be among the people who achieve that small chance of success.

That belief is what makes entrepreneurs, by nature, optimists. In one survey of 3,000 entrepreneurs who had recently become business owners 81 percent believed that their chances of success were 70 percent or higher. A third even believed that they were 100 percent certain to succeed. Optimism is a characteristic that's been found in entrepreneurs in research study after research study. In one paper, researchers found that only 5 percent of entrepreneurs underestimate the course of their new company's development. More than 50 percent overestimate it. In fact, typically 70 percent of new businesses fail within four years. The entrepreneur knows this stat but will forge ahead anyway and it's the reason there are so many great new businesses as well. That's the part the entrepreneur sees. The new business, the new success, the new life—and they know they can do it.

That optimism isn't spread evenly. Entrepreneurs who are bringing to life a completely new idea or starting their own businesses tend to be more optimistic than people who are entering a crowded market or taking over an existing firm. Entrepreneurs with less experience in their field of activity tend to be less optimistic than people with more experience. And men are generally more optimistic than women are, which is another way of saying that men are more likely to overestimate their abilities.

Confidence is necessary for any entrepreneur but overconfidence can be dangerous. An experiment conducted in 2006 found unrealistic optimism causes entrepreneurs to behave in ways that harm their best own best interests; both professionally and personally. That confidence and optimism can lead an entrepreneur to continue trying, investing and making sacrifices long after it's become clear that the venture is failing. What psychologists call "optimistic cognitive bias" can lead entrepreneurs to overestimate demand, underestimate the competition, and fail to see the need for complementary assets.

Optimism and overconfidence are the two most commonly reported causes of the high failure rates of new businesses. In one study as many as half of inventors with ideas described as "very poor quality" continued to pursue their efforts even when paid advice argued strongly against it. This may be one clue for the entrepreneur to take to heart. Paid advice. The entrepreneur will need to get advice from someone who is an expert in the field that they are entering. Even if the entrepreneur is an expert themselves, outside input from a trusted person is a must.

Generally, outside input has to be paid for and unbiased, it's not from mom or your friends nor your roommates. That is not to say that the "expert" cannot be incorrect. They can. Sometimes you have to do what you have to do and too bad what anyone else says. However, if a true expert is questioning the idea of the product or service itself you need to take a much closer look and give greater weight to your considerations and testing.

When entrepreneurs believe in their own abilities, their optimism can become self-fulfilling prophecies. Some research has shown that optimistic entrepreneurs perform better and more competitively in many circumstances. Optimism is what helps to drive entrepreneurs towards success, overcome their failures and focus on solutions and possibilities rather than on the setbacks and problems. It's what enables entrepreneurs to get things done and usually done more quickly.

And, entrepreneurs may well be right. A study in Sweden looked at survey data collected between 1996 and 2009 in which Swedish citizens were asked whether they thought the economy *had* improved over the last twelve months, and if they thought it *would* improve over the next twelve months.

Not surprisingly, entrepreneurs were more optimistic about the state of the economy than other respondents were. But they were also more accurate than other respondents; their predictions of the future course of the economy tended to more closely match what actually happened. The researchers went on to argue that while entrepreneurs are usually described as overly-optimistic, to have too much faith in their own abilities and be unwilling to face the facts about the chances of success, regular wage-earners actually tend to have outlooks that are too bleak.

"Entrepreneurs make smaller forecast errors than non-entrepreneurs," the study said. "[They] view the future as bright—but they are actually right. Our evidence thereby challenges the prevailing argument that entrepreneurs are irrational in how they form their beliefs about the future. Rather, it is non-entrepreneurs who are more irrational, because their beliefs are overly pessimistic."

Every entrepreneur starts a new business with the awareness that they might fail but also the belief that they have the skills and the determination and the personality to succeed. Some of those entrepreneurs may be proved wrong—this time. But all entrepreneurs have that faith in themselves and they're right to keep it. The faith in themselves also means that, though they may fail one time it doesn't mean they will fail the next time. This extra push and effort on behalf of oneself is what sets the entrepreneur apart from the rest of the population. An entrepreneur knows how to pick themselves up, dust themselves off and run. An entrepreneur does not wallow. Wallowing allows too much time for self-pity. Entrepreneurs have little patience for this type of attitude or action from themselves or from others who may be around them.

21

Your Passion Is Infectious

Dave Nevogt had an idea. It was February 2012, and the serial entrepreneur thought there might be a market for time-tracking software that companies could use to manage their remote staff. He knew he couldn't create it himself. His background was in marketing and management; he knew nothing about Ruby On Rails or desktop development. But he didn't just want to hire a coder. He wanted a partner, a co-founder who would take on the responsibility of building a new business with him and share the load with him. "There were things I didn't feel comfortable taking ownership of and that's why I went to find a co-founder," Nevogt wrote in a blog post at Hubspot, the company he would create.

Often, co-founders are old friends. They might be former colleagues who dream up an idea together or they could be old college mates who start playing around after class and find that they're developing something that's got legs.

However, that doesn't always happen. Sometimes entrepreneurs have an idea but don't know anyone who can help them to develop it. When that happens they have to persuade someone to join them. It's not just a matter of offering a larger salary; it's the other person's ability to share a vision, to infect someone else with the same passion that they feel for the path they want to follow.

In his blog post, Nevogt explains how he went about tracking down and recruiting—not a staff member—but a co-founder who would work with him to build a new business from scratch.

He started by looking on LinkedIn for developers in his area who met four criteria:

- They could show that they had completed a product.
- They were business-minded.
- They had management experience.
- They were local.

Those aren't all the criteria that an entrepreneur looks for in an employee and they may not be your criteria. But take a moment and write down what qualities you must have in your startup which will compliment your strengths. Hired coders don't have to be business-minded; they just have to be focused and skilled. But a co-founder needs to make business decisions as well as write code and lead a development team.

Nevogt wrote to a few people he found on LinkedIn, explaining that he was looking for a good developer. He shared the link to the company's website and suggested setting up a time to call. Jared Brown, who would become the company's CTO and co-founder, took twelve days to answer and when he did, indicated that he was only interested in "entertaining remote contract opportunities."

Nevogt, though, wasn't put off by the lengthier response time, nor by this answer. In fact, he appears to have been encouraged by it. "You want your potential partner to ask questions and take everything into consideration. Smart people should need to be talked into doing stuff, especially developers. Building a new product from the ground up is no easy task, and whoever comes aboard should know what they're getting into in terms of work and commitment."

The two finally talked on the phone, and they met for dinner. They drew up responsibility lists and Nevogt convinced Brown with two things: data and experience. He brought data showing that there was a market for the product they were creating and he brought evidence that showed the cost of customer acquisition. Nevogt was able to show that he had created a similar white-label product in the past and that he had created companies that had generated a million dollars in revenues. Finally, he offered Brown a 50-50 split. "I knew this amount of ownership would be motivating because it would be just as much his business as mine."

Those were all important factors and they would have helped to persuade Brown that he was looking at an opportunity not another freelance client. But we all see or think of lots of opportunities every day. What makes the difference between the opportunities we accept and the opportunities we spurn is the passion we feel for them—and that's what Nevogt passed on to Brown when they spoke on the phone and met for dinner.

That ability to create partnerships out of charm and drive is part of every entrepreneur. When an entrepreneur believes in their idea, they have the ability to spread that faith. The people they talk to come to share their vision and when they believe in the entrepreneur's ability to create that vision, they come to share their passion too. There is nothing more exciting than the feeling that comes when you're building something new and you believe—*you know*—that it's going to be huge.

When an entrepreneur talks about their plan with passion, their audience doesn't just see it. They feel that passion, and they can envision their part in building it. They *want* to be a part of it.

Entrepreneurs are sociable and they pull in people around them because they offer an opportunity to others to be part of something great. Passion can be infectious, and a good entrepreneur with a great idea spreads that infection everywhere they go.

22

You Think The Right Response To An Order Is A Question

Walk through a neighborhood and you can always tell which houses are occupied by owners and which contain renters. The owner-occupied homes have tidy front yards. There are usually some plants and trees. The place is dressed-up. There are no cracks in the walls and the sidewalk at the end of the drive is always clean and swept. Trash isn't littering the place. Owners care about their property and they maintain it. When they see a problem, they don't let it fester because they know that they're responsible for it. When damage grows, so does the bill and it will always land on them and no one else.

Renters don't pay the repair bills and they don't lose money if the property falls in value so they seldom if ever take the initiative. If a renter sees the walls cracking around them they'll ignore it. If a pipe leaks, then they might call the landlord, unless they feel they can live with the dripping, in which case they'll be happy to avoid picking up the phone. Small problems become large problems, the extent of damages grow, and the cost of repairs when the tenant finally moves out is greater than it would have been if the repairman had been called about at the first sign of trouble or the plumber had fixed the leak after the first drip.

Entrepreneurs often see their employees in the same way. Renters feel that the company isn't theirs so it doesn't matter to them if the product is poor or the service they deliver to customers is more insulting than helpful. When they see a problem, they might tell a manager and leave it to someone else to fix but they're more likely to just ignore it. Their job is to stack the shelves or answer the phone; no one told them anything about picking up fallen products or answering customers' questions. Their attitude about seeing a fault in a product is "it's not my problem." I am often amazed when I am consulting in a business, and I point out a true potential hazard to a business and the person merely shrugs their shoulder's as if asking, "so why are you telling me?" I know right then, this person has a renter's mentality and doesn't care about the business they are working in.

An entrepreneur might not own the company but they act like they do. When they see a problem in the company, they don't just alert a manager, they offer a plan to fix it, and where possible, they just fix it themselves or call someone in to fix the problem. When a customer makes a complaint, they don't just pass that complaint along; they follow up, make sure the issue was settled and check with the customer to make certain that they're satisfied.

The biggest difference between renters and owners in a company though, comes when an entrepreneur receives instructions. Renters don't rebel. They do what they're told, *exactly* what they're told, and no more. If they're asked to clean the warehouse or write a script, they'll clean the warehouse or write the script. Then, they'll stop and wait to be told what to do next. They won't ask themselves why the warehouse needs to be cleaned or what the script is for. If the renter employee sees that the instruction wasn't completely clear or failed to take into account an issue their manager hadn't considered, they won't bother to look for a solution. It's not their job.

An owner does see the big picture. As they're cleaning the warehouse, they'll make sure they leave space for whatever is supposed to come into the warehouse next. They'll leave a record of where they've put everything in the warehouse so that anyone can find the supplies. When they've finished their job, they'll look for something else to organize without waiting to be told. The coder wouldn't just write the script, he'd also test it and think about the different environments in which this script could be used, making sure that it can run anywhere. He thinks like the owner of the company, anticipating problems and trying to solve them before they come up.

However, an entrepreneur is neither an owner-employee nor a renter-employee. An entrepreneur is no kind of employee at all. When they're working for a company and see a problem, they'll fix it because it needs to be fixed but that's never enough. They'll want to know why that problem was there in the first place, how did the problem occur, when was the problem first noted and by whom, whether other companies suffer from this same problem and whether anyone is offering to help those companies fix them.

When a customer complains, an entrepreneur will deal with the issue and get back to the customer to make sure everything is okay, but then they'll wonder what it would take to move that customer to another business and they'll make a quick count of other customers who could be pried away from this business and can form the base of a new firm.

When an entrepreneur receives an instruction, they'll understand what the company is trying to do but instead of getting on with it and completing it in a way that allows the project to move forward, they'll wonder whether the project is moving in the right direction. They'll ask questions and they won't accept answers that aren't satisfactory. They'll point out a better way to meet the goal and they'll insist that they're right because there's a good chance they are.

This attitude can be somewhat irritating to some managers and business owners. Instead of seeing the value in this person's exceptional mind and effort, they think it is a criticism of their business instead of a help. Some managers even get offended at the efforts of these entrepreneurs.

I have seen entrepreneurs at work in someone else's company and it is down right discouraging to see. They want so much to make a difference to the company and to help grow something, and they are like a puppy dog. And, those managers and owner's who can't see this longing really miss out on a huge opportunity to help grow the company in a meaningful way.

What I've found quite comical, on occasion, is how much money the managers and owners miss by way of free labor. The entrepreneur heart will work overtime for nothing in the benefit of a really good cause even if it's not their own. That is until they find out they are underappreciated (and generally not just underappreciated—berated and "adjusted" in what they are doing), and they get smart.

Therefore, the attitude of an entrepreneur in someone else's business certainly isn't as small-minded as the outlook of a renter-employee. But it's also not as helpful and co-operative as the work of an owner-employee. It's the kind of resistance that often leads to office rows, and eventually a sacking.

Entrepreneurs don't take instructions extremely well, from anyone; they give instructions and they look for the big-thinking employees who make those instructions happen. Until they own their own companies, they're always going to be a point of friction in a firm, and yet a source of bright ideas for the intuitive businessperson who will take and use those helps and suggestions in the way in which the offering is given.

23

You Only Feel Job Security
When You're The Boss

During the last recession, American companies laid off 8.7 million people. Those people worked in occupations that ranged from Wall Street banking to Detroit car-making. They had flipped burgers, sold properties, designed websites, written code, assisted dentists, calculated actuarial rates and performed every other task found in every city across America.

Some of those people would have been new at their work. They'll have started the new jobs, expecting to stay in them for years, pocketing a regular pay check and enjoying a stable income. Others will already have put their time into the company. They might have thought they'd be able to work their way up the ranks, increasing their salaries and looking forward to a happy retirement. They would have been shocked to find that they now have to dust off their résumés and start again. They might even have believed at that time, that they never would find another job.

In fact, whether those workers who received their P45s during the last recession had just landed their positions or whether they had been in the corner office for years, few should really have expected to stay with the same company for a long time. In 2014, the median tenure at any job was just 4.6 years, a figure that hadn't changed since the U.S. Bureau of Labor's previous survey two years earlier. Even in management positions it's just 5.7 years, and while the median tenure of workers aged between 55 and 64 is 10.4 years, employees aged between 25 and 34 can expect to stay with the same company for just three years.

Some of that job-changing will be voluntary. Young people, especially Millennials, have little problem moving around. If the Gen Y see an opportunity at another company that beats anything available in their own firm, they'll be happy to jump ship. But much of the job insecurity that employees face is involuntary. They get laid off. They're fired, made redundant, or replaced by cheaper workers in far-off countries.

The reasons that employees lose their jobs can vary considerably. Sometimes, it will be the result of behavior the company doesn't condone. Fail to make it into work on time too frequently, regardless of how many hours you work or how productive you are in the hours you're at your desk, and you can expect that call into the manager's office.

Rub a colleague the wrong way and he can tell people that you're hard to work with and need to be replaced. Vent on social media about a decision that you can see is wrong, and you can be told that if you can't get with the program you have to get out. Ignore an instruction that you think is a waste of time and you can find yourself spending more time looking for another position. The point is, in someone else's business, you do the job the way they have told you to do it.

In one job I was in, the manager said I came in late. I don't know how the manager would know if I had come in late or not, because he was never there and he had taken most of the previous four months off. Of the 50 employees in the office, I was the only one who actually came in close to the opening hour and we all worked many, many hours of unpaid overtime because we were salaried, and we wanted to help each other succeed.

Perhaps the most common reason that employees are laid off is that the manager thinks they've put in a poor performance. That can happen, and it can even happen to entrepreneurs. People whose natural position is to make decisions and delegate work rather than to accept instructions and perform small tasks make for poor employees. When someone has been hired to do nothing more than test scripts or answer phones, their manager will see their questions and their opinions as obstacles that get in the way of the smooth running of the firm.

There is no such thing today as a secure job. All jobs are insecure, and no career now starts with a post-school apprenticeship and continues through salary rises all the way to a comfortable retirement. Those days are long gone, if they ever existed at all.

Entrepreneurs understand this better than anyone else. They feel it more than anyone else. They know that as long as they have a boss, they do not have complete control over their own lives. One mistake can result in someone else making a decision that they can't influence and which would change the way they live. As an employee, they're never more than one phone call away from the complete loss of their income, a complete change in their colleagues and an entirely different way of working.

That doesn't mean that being an entrepreneur will bring security. It won't. It will bring *less* security. In the early months of the business, the company will have to battle to find its niche and land customers. Every day the business survives will feel like a victory. Every salary withdrawal will feel like a miracle. Every lost customer will feel like a disaster.

Even if the company survives and prospers, once it obtains a board of governors, the founder's position is no more secure than that of an employee. In a world in which even Steve Jobs can be handed a P45, every chief executive understands that they always have other people to please.

The difference is control. Entrepreneurs aren't fired at a whim. A single mistake or even a series of small mistakes is rarely enough to get them canned. As long as the company is growing and profits are rising, the entrepreneur's position will be safe. And the entrepreneur gets to make the decisions that determine whether the company grows or fails.

No one has job security, but entrepreneurs have control and they have confidence. As long as they're in charge of the company, they're in charge of their destiny. And, that's as secure a feeling as anyone can hope to enjoy.

24

You Want To Be The Captain
Not The Admiral

n 1917, with the First World War still raging, carmaker Rolls-Royce
found itself under pressure to merge with the armaments company
Vickers. The board asked Henry Royce, the engineer who had co-
founded the company, for his opinion about the two firms combining.
After considering in his reply the state of the luxury car market in the
post-war years and describing the benefits of the merger for "economy
of selling, manufacture and technical management," Royce described his
own preference. "From a personal point of view, I prefer to be absolute
boss over my own department (even if it was extremely small) rather
than to be associated with a much larger technical department over
which I had only joint control," he wrote.

For Royce, control was everything. He insisted on seeing every design drawn up by the company's engineers and draughtsmen. (A draughtsmen is more than a draftsman; they are qualified to draw mechanical drawings in differing detailed scales from the first screw to the last bolt—in precise order of usability.) Royce had to *see* *every piece* of the item being built and even tried to return to the factory immediately after surgery when he had been given just a few days to live.

It's a preference that every entrepreneur understands. Every business starts as an idea in an entrepreneur's mind, a vision of a product and a company that, with the right skill, determination and hard work can become real.

When it does become real, beating all the doubters who said it couldn't happen and all the critics who predicted failure, there are always two reactions.

The first is a boost in confidence. The entrepreneur was the only one who believed not just in their vision but in their ability to make that vision real. They've been proved right. If they ever had any doubts before, a look at the product and the sales figures goes a long way to removing any doubts that remain.

The other reaction is to then believe that *only* they can continue to make that vision happen. Only they can approve the design. Only they can develop the marketing strategy. Only they can choose the company's message and its branding. Only they can set not just the company's direction but oversee the work of its engineers and its managers and the rest of its staff.

Having built success with their own hands, they believe that only with their hands on the product can the company continue to produce that success.

They're not always right. Writing in the *Harvard Business Review*, Noam Wasserman described how founder-CEOs begin by wanting both wealth and power. They want their company to be worth billions and they want to continue to control every aspect of it.

In the early days of the company, those two choices are rarely in conflict. Before the product ships, the company has little money and is small enough to be easily managed. But once the product is out of the door and the firm starts to look for funds from investors to grow more quickly, the entrepreneur has to decide whether he wants to be the captain of the ship or the admiral of the fleet.

Each option has its advantages and its disadvantages. Being captain means giving up power. In one survey of 212 US start-ups that began operating in the late nineties and early 2000s, Wasserman found that by the time the companies were three years old, only half of the founders were still the CEO. A year later, that figure had fallen by 10 percent, and by the time the companies had an IPO, three-quarters were no longer led by their founders.

Not all of those changes would have been voluntary. Some entrepreneurs insist that they need to be in control of everything even as a board that they no longer control points out that the skills required to imagine and create a company are not the same as the skills required to grow and manage a large corporation. The battles would have been painful and the end result is likely to be have been a complete parting of the ways. Wasserman argues that entrepreneurs who try to retain both wealth and power end up with neither.

"The surprising thing is that trying to maximize one imperils achievement of the other," he writes. "Entrepreneurs face a choice, at every step, between making money and managing their ventures. Those who don't figure out which is more important to them often end up neither wealthy nor powerful."

Smart entrepreneurs understand that when companies grow and become valuable, it often happens because the founder has chosen to retain control over those elements of the firm where they can contribute the most. Instead of trying to be both chairman of the board and chief executive officer, they hire a board of people they trust and they listen to their advice.

They might even look for a chief executive with business and management experience to keep an eye on the share price while they focus on the engineering or the design. The result is that the equity that they hold in the company continues to grow, while they contain to influence those parts of the firm that mean the most to them, and to the firm's success.

After explaining his own preference for strong control in a small department over joint control in a large department, Henry Royce advised the board to ignore his opinion. "This ought *not* be considered," he wrote. "We [will] endeavor to work together."

Royce was an entrepreneur. He let the board decide the future of the firm he had helped to create. He wanted control but he understood that sometimes you have to give up some power for the sake of the business and to retain control where it matters most.

25

You Can't Toss A Rock Without Hitting An Opportunity

How often has someone told you that they have a great idea for a business? And, how often has that person been an employee, earning a salary and working for someone else?

You've probably walked away from that conversation completely confused. If they think their idea is so great, why aren't they doing anything about it? And, if they really see themselves as an entrepreneur-in-waiting, why are they so proud of themselves for having an idea? Entrepreneurs have a dozen different ideas before breakfast.

The difference between an entrepreneur and the average working Joe isn't that one can see an opportunity that the other misses entirely. It's that an entrepreneur can see opportunities everywhere—then sort through them, understand what it would take to make one work and finally roll up their sleeves to make it happen.

Because opportunity really is everywhere and new chances appear every day. Ask an entrepreneur where they got the idea for their business from, and you'll hear as many different answers as there are companies. In general, though, opportunities tend to come from three sources.

The first is a solution to a problem that they've experienced personally. When an entrepreneur receives poor customer service, they start to wonder whether there isn't a better way to provide after-sales care. When they reverse into a bollard that they couldn't see in the mirror, they wonder whether it would be possible to put sensors or a camera in the rear fender that can warn them when they're getting too close. When they find themselves wasting time organizing their invoices or collecting tax receipts, they start thinking about a product that could save them a headache—and save other people a headache too.

David Cohen, founder and CEO of Techstars, (in Boulder, CO) for example, explained to the *Wall Street Journal*, that he created one of his companies after struggling to find news about the music he loved. EarFeeder would check users' computers for the music they had already purchased then build a news stream from the Internet based on their preferences, together with ticket deals and special offers.

When an entrepreneur encounters a problem, they always walk away with an opportunity.

The second source of opportunities are the problems that they can see other people experiencing. That's a bigger challenge. It's easy enough to feel your own frustration but it takes sympathy and understanding to realize that the frustration someone else feels isn't a personality issue or something that affects only one person but a business opportunity that could bring benefits to many people.

Jennifer Hyman's inspiration for creating Rent the Runway wasn't her own concern about the state of her wardrobe; it was staying with her sister during a break from Harvard Business School, and seeing that her sister had just spent a fortune on a dress for a wedding even though she had a closet full of other choices. Realizing that social media was making women less willing to wear the same outfit twice, she spotted an opportunity that could solve her sister's problem, and everyone else's.

The third common source of a business opportunity is new technology. Every time technology takes a step forward, it gives entrepreneurs a case full of new tools that they can use to solve a host of different problems. So when Apple opened the App Store, it gave entrepreneurs a solution to the problem of bringing a video game to market. In the past, games designers had needed to print CDs, design packaging and deliver the box sets to stores across the country. Now they only needed to write the code and submit it to the store.

The release of the device itself created all sorts of new opportunities, from apps that turned the device into a flashlight to apps that made rude noises. For an entrepreneur, the question is never where to look to find an opportunity. Those opportunities are never more than a stone's throw away. An entrepreneur can't walk into a building without estimating its value, wondering about the companies behind the doors and assuming that those businesses have problems that need solving and budgets to buy a product that they could create for them.

The challenge for an entrepreneur is how to assess all of the opportunities that they can see, and choose the ones with the best chance of success.

Just as opportunity itself comes from a variety of different sources and in multiple forms, so the ways in which entrepreneurs choose them vary too. Some entrepreneurs just follow their heart. They pick the idea that burns the brightest and run with it. Others do the market research. They compare competitors, a few might even conduct focus groups, and they take the opportunity that looks like it has the greatest chance of success.

Some entrepreneurs, like Jeff Bezos, will prefer the choice that can bring the biggest rewards, however long it takes to win them while others will apply the maxim of being able to fail fast and cheaply. They'll take the opportunity that costs the least and will show quickly whether it can work.

What entrepreneurs never do though is get excited about a single idea nor do they tell strangers about the best ideas they've had. They don't talk about those opportunities. They take them and move on them.

26

You Take Personality Tests— And Wonder How To Monetize Them

For General Ne Win, the dictator who ruled Burma for 26 years, numbers were everything. Nine was his lucky number so he made sure that important events were staged on dates whose numbers could be added together to make nine. In 1987, he ordered that all banknotes should be divisible by nine. Notes worth 45 kyats and 90 kyats replaced 50 and 100-kyat notes, wiping out savings and making cash payments difficult.

Few entrepreneurs are that superstitious. They don't trust the likes of lucky numbers or the stars or consult the lines on their hands before making important financial decisions. Entrepreneurs know they're in control of their own destinies. Fate doesn't deliver success; only hard work, drive and a willingness to take risks does that.

But, entrepreneurs do understand that even if their future isn't written in the stars it might be written in their genes. It takes a special kind of person to create their own business. It takes a rare kind of person to create their own business. There are far more employees and far more people willing to remain employees than there are people with the determination to turn a business idea into a successful company.

Entrepreneurs always want to be certain that they are indeed that kind of person.

Because it is easy to doubt, success never comes overnight. It only ever comes after a long series of nights, many of them short and even more of them sleepless. Until the business is up and running, any entrepreneur, even the most confident and well-supported one will wonder at times whether they really do have what it takes to find the funding, hire the staff, produce the marketing plans and deliver the product. They will wonder if they're really an entrepreneur or just someone who at one time thought they might be.

Until this questioning entrepreneur has the corner office and the bank balance and the name on the building that proves that they really are who they think they are, personality tests that can tell them about their characters can always look tempting. There's no shortage of them. The Myer-Briggs test often tells entrepreneurs that they're ENTP, a personality type that focuses on action but also likes to think through problems. They challenge the status quo, prefer new ideas and avoid structures that limit and restrain them.

Entrepreneurs who take tests offered by the Enneagram Institute might discover that they're "reformers," or people who tend to control their anger and their emotions. They like to direct their energies inwards, to their inner critic, resolving their imperfections and constantly looking to improve themselves.

Others will use much simpler form of personality theory and assume that they're Type A: competitive, outgoing and ambitious.

Entrepreneurs might take these tests occasionally but they're also aware of their limitations. The Myers-Briggs tests are notoriously complex with overlapping patterns of characteristics. The action-driven ENTP entrepreneurs could just as easily be multi-functional ENFPs, order-giving ENTJs, inventive INTJs or creative INTPs. An entrepreneur could just as easily be the Enneagram Institutes, "achiever" or "individualist" as its "reformer."

Anyone who's already taken steps to build a business has already proved that they have the characteristics that make up a Type A personality, but I've been a witness to incredible other personality types who have become entrepreneur's, or have partnered with the Type A's.

There is in all of these tests a degree of confirmation bias. When we're looking for a reason to believe that we're on the right track, passing a test that tells us we're the right person for the path ahead is always comforting. And the results are usually vague enough for us to interpret them in a way that does exactly that: whether a personality test tells that we're purposeful or adaptable, self-controlled or self-absorbed, it's never too difficult to take that description and apply it to the personality of a successful entrepreneur.

Taking personality tests does something else too. The Myers-Briggs test was invented by a mother and daughter in the 1940s and eventually went on to become the best-selling product sold by a psychology press in California. The Enneagram Institute isn't just a personality test; it's a product that requires marketing and depends on its branding to pull in customers and win evangelists. And those evangelists work hard. They spread the word of the test they've taken to their friends, recommending it with a strength that other businesses can only dream of.

Entrepreneurs take personality tests to reassure themselves that they really were born for a life of leadership and development. But as they think about those tests, they also analyze the institute's business growth, its marketing and the way it has managed to attract customers and sell its main product.

Entrepreneurs understand that success is never down to who they are; it's always down to what they do. And when they take a personality test, they recognize the work of someone else who did manage to turn an idea into a business.

Taking a personality test and thinking about how that entrepreneur managed to sell it to you is a stronger sign that you were born to be a business leader than the numbers, colors, alphabet letter, or label which is identified in the test results. Test away. It's kind of fun.

Testing has also helped me identify some actual or potential traits in employees and business partners that can benefit the company and they are traits that I hadn't noticed before nor seen as desirable and helpful. But having these traits pointed out has made me realize that they are *really* desirable and I surely want to encourage these attributes in my employees and business partners—so I've take notice.

27

You Ignore The Problems
And Look For Solutions

f Michael O'Leary, the founder of budget airline RyanAir, ever takes
a look at his company's Facebook page, he'd be unlikely to enjoy the
experience. Posts made by the firm's social media team cover topics
that range from flying information to pictures of beautiful locations.
Comments, though, take just two forms: customers either ask for
information about a flight they're about to take or they complain about
a flight they've already taken.

It's a pattern seen across airline pages, and across the pages of other
businesses. When customers talk to a brand it's usually to say something
negative. Good service is taken for granted while disappointing
experiences are trumpeted far and wide.

Complaining is not a behavior pattern of entrepreneurs. It is a characteristic of employees, and, in particular, employees who don't have to take the responsibility of solving issues. My own personality has always been to skip past the complaining part, and go straight for the fix of what is bothering me, part.

Problems are always easy to spot and much harder to fix. That's why software companies invest giant sums in their development teams but give beta testers nothing in return for their bug-spotting but a sneak peek at the next release. Almost anyone can see when something is wrong. But you need special skills to make something wrong—right.

It's also satisfying to identify problems. See an issue that's damaging a firm, whether it's the rudeness of the staff or a feature that doesn't quite work for the company, and someone who didn't work on it, knows nothing about how to build it and was never invited to share their opinion about it, gets to feel clever. They might not be the chief executive or the founder, but they can see something someone far more successful than them has missed.

It's the same sense of satisfaction that has the bar lizards solving crises in the Middle East over a glass of beer and a bowl of nuts while international diplomats with decades of experience struggle to make any headway. Focusing on a problem is simple. Dreaming up a solution that will never be tested through implementation is fun.

Actually figuring out a solution that needs to be built, financed, tested and implemented, and identifying for which someone this product or service is needed, takes a lot of responsibility, and it takes the effort and energy of an entrepreneur.

It's not that entrepreneurs don't see problems. They see them, then they look for the opportunity that the problem provides. Because the solution to any problem is always a new opportunity. It's a chance to make an improvement, beat a competitor or tie a customer closer to the company. It's a chance to move forward, sell more and make a bigger mark in their chosen field. The instinct of any entrepreneur is first to spot the problem, but instead of relaxing and enjoying the satisfaction of seeing something that others have missed, they start to think about how to fix the problem.

That's where things start to get a lot harder. Whenever someone begins voicing their opinion with the words, "I don't understand..." they're always right. They don't understand. Whether they go on to say, "...why they don't just send in the Marines and finish them off," or, "... why doesn't Apple just launch its television already," they don't understand the complexities involved in implementing their solution. And they don't really care about implementation. What they really care about is voicing their opinion and using that opinion to show who they are, and sometimes they just want to recreationally complain.

Entrepreneurs don't have that luxury, and they don't want that luxury. They don't want the satisfaction that comes from merely seeing a problem, they want the satisfaction of identifying a solution that would work and seeing it work once it's implemented.

That requires a very different way of thinking. It means initially putting aside emotion and looking coldly at the problem. It means asking why the problem exists, what benefits the current way of working brings about and examining how it's possible to retain those benefits while still removing the problem.

It also means accepting the reality that sometimes it's not possible to do everything. One of the most common questions in job interviews is "What's your biggest weakness?" The most common smartass answer is, "I'm a perfectionist." This is aggravating to employers and the potential employees who gives this response is really revealing a weakness because entrepreneurs know that nothing is ever perfect. Every product that rolls out of the company is the result of compromise. Budgets and deadlines limit how far developers can go. Pricing limits mean that designers have to work with parts that might not be the best available. The need to appeal to a broad market can mean pulling back on some features and adding others that some people will never use.

Every product has a problem. Every product can generate complaints. And every product can inspire someone to post on Facebook or begin a conversation with a shake of the head and the words "I don't understand..."

It's frustrating for a company founder to look at their Facebook page, their emails or their support forums and see the lists of complaints and feature requests. They know how much effort went into creating the features that those customers *do* enjoy. And they know why their products come short in some areas while excelling in others. Not only do they see the problem, they understand it, and they're always looking for practical ways to solve it.

Several incredible entrepreneurs, such as Oprah Winfrey, have revealed that they don't even read their social media themselves because it's too damaging to their soul. They hire others to read the media and then they deal with opinions which must be dealt with. The "haters"— well, we'll save that topic for another day. The entrepreneur doesn't have time for that kind of heavy baggage, unless they can find a way to make money from it, or make a company from it.

28

You Know The Difference Between An Idea And A Product

L ife for people who aren't entrepreneurs always contains a certain amount of frustration. Entrepreneurs aren't the only ones who can see opportunities. Other people may find opportunities in unusual places. They may find more of them. They may be thinking about them all of the time. But even people who will spend their lives working for someone else and can be content to work that way will still have business ideas and see gaps in the market. They'll still have those moments when they think, "Why has no one built that?" And after a longer delay than that felt by an entrepreneur perhaps, they'll wonder and think and take time to wonder some more about whether they could do that.

For someone who isn't an entrepreneur, that's where the process will stop because someone who has never seen themselves as anything other than a small cog in a large machine doesn't understand the difference between an idea and a product. They think that having an idea is the hard part, that the concept is what makes a business valuable.

Entrepreneurs know different. They know the real difference between an idea and a product. They understand that the idea is barely even half a step down a long road that will lead to success. It's a necessary step. It's the step that defines the direction of the business and gives it a goal. But it's not really even a forward movement.

Entrepreneurs understand that the difference between an idea and a product isn't the power of the idea or the size of the market. It's execution. People who aren't entrepreneurs have good ideas and they wonder why those ideas don't leap out of their heads and turn themselves into products right in front of them. Entrepreneurs know that those ideas remain figments of the imagination until someone puts in the effort to turn them into something physical. And, oh, it takes work.

When someone who isn't an entrepreneur has a good idea for an app, for a product, for a service or for any other business, they congratulate themselves on their smart thinking and their ability to spot an opportunity. When an entrepreneur has an idea for a business, they quickly start thinking about how the execution would take place. What challenges would a venture like this reveal, and how would those problems need to be overcome?

Those challenges usually take three forms.

The first is money. Every business idea requires cash to start rolling. When an entrepreneur has an idea, their experience will start to give them an estimate of the amount of money needed to get started. That first estimate won't be perfect, but it will still be pretty accurate for the start. They'll be able to come up with a ball-park figure that can take an idea from the mind, if not into the market, and at least into development.

That's the first thought, and it's an empowering one because the problem of raising funds has a solution. There are always funds available for great business ideas. Entrepreneurs just have to persuade the people with their fingers on the purse-strings to open them up. As soon as an entrepreneur recognizes that the first barrier between an idea and a product is price, things start to move forward because that barrier can be knocked down. A successful entrepreneur may have some of their own funds that can carry them through the first months of research and business planning and writing. They may start to mentally list investors they know who would want to put money into an idea like this one. They'll wonder how much they could raise in a Kickstarter campaign and what sort of benefits they'd need to offer.

In short, as soon as they start thinking about the problem of money, they start thinking of financial solutions. And once those possible solutions start to break that barrier down, the excitement of winning pushes them towards the next barrier: development.

The development of the product itself may be difficult. It's possible that the entrepreneur will be able to do some of the work themselves. If an entrepreneur with a background in coding has an idea for an app, they can start putting the code together and building the database. Even before any work has been done they'll be mentally blocking off hours at the weekend to get the first version up and running. But few successful products are ever made by one person so she'll need to call in help from a designer and a composer and a script writer.

As those problems pop-up, the entrepreneur thinks through solutions. They start to identify people they know who know other people who can help. Initially, that help might be freelance but that could be enough to turn an idea into a prototype.

Already the path from concept to construction is starting to open: the money will come from this source and that savings account; the work can come in those hours and from those professionals. This will just leave the marketing, but having thought this far for the product or service, an entrepreneur will feel a burning urge to check out competitors, gain a greater understanding of their customers and look for the flaws in their own products that they can repair and overcome right now while it's easier.

When people who aren't entrepreneurs have business ideas, they think they've done the hard work and they're left, years later, wondering why that idea still hasn't somehow materialized and made them rich.

When entrepreneurs have a strong business idea, within a few days, that idea will have morphed into an opportunity. After a week or two, it's a plan. A few months later, that plan has become a project and some months after that, it might just be a product. An entrepreneur understands all of the activity that makes the difference between burst of inspiration and a business that inspires.

29

You Always Reach The Finish Line, Even If You Have To Draw It Yourself

In the technology industry, the mean life span of a failing start-up after its last funding round is about 20 months. The median time from funding round to failure is 16.5 months. That's much shorter than many owners of a new business might prefer. An entrepreneur can pass very quickly from the joy of receiving a seven-figure check from investors impressed by their business plan to the misery of checking that the office door is locked when they leave the building for the last time. Believe me, this stinks. But you jump up and move again, quickly.

Entrepreneurs know that their plans can only end in one of three ways. The company they're building could grow and grow and keep on growing until it takes over the world, has offices in every major capital and can buys its own island retreat for its executives somewhere in the Caribbean, together with a corporate jet to whisk them there.

It might also end with a buyout. Someone from Google or Facebook or Exxon will come up to them at a conference and enquire if they've ever thought of selling. There will be meetings and negotiations, provisions will be laid out for employees and eventually the figures will be released before the entrepreneur takes a large check, maybe buys a bigger house and starts a new business for fun this time, instead of out of a need to make a living.

Of course, there's that third way: the moment when it's clear that bills can't be paid, expenses are greater than revenues, and now it's time to cut the cord and lay off the employees. This is extremely painful but it's also an opportunity to throw off something that's been dragging you (and your family) down for some time, and now you can start something new and hopeful.

All of those moments are endings, and all the endings are personal and imposed on the entrepreneur. The moments have to be began or ended by the entrepreneurs, but they don't give up. An entrepreneur will just keep going until they reach one of those endings. Even if the way ahead looks tough and growth is slow at the moment, as long as there's hope that things can improve, an entrepreneur will keep plugging away, looking to launch new products and hoping that the next project is that one that will takes off.

The problem is that this scenario above doesn't always happen. There is a fourth destiny for companies started by entrepreneurs: they can become zombie companies. These are firms that drift along. They make just enough money to pay the bills but never enough to invest in new products. They pay the interest on their debts but never enough to lower the principal. They can't employ new staff or raise salaries but they can meet payroll and keep people on board.

It's a problem that affects a great number of companies. Company Watch, a British risk management firm, estimates that the UK alone had 227,000 companies with liabilities of at least £5,000 more than their assets at the end of 2013. Their combined deficits amounted to more than £70 billion.

For an entrepreneur, it's the worst possible situation. On the one hand they've achieved something, and it's something more than most people ever come close to achieving. They've turned an idea into a business, made a product that people want to buy, and did the marketing that brought them customers. That's already made them a success.

Most entrepreneurs want and need more than the zombie existence. If they were content with that level of operation, they'd open a mom-and-pop grocery store and pocket the cash. While that's a perfectly reasonable degree of entrepreneurship, when most people start a business now, they're looking for something more. They don't just want one store, they want many. They don't want to spend their days standing behind a counter or sitting at a desk taking orders, they want to be able to employ people to work for them so that they can can provide for many others, and so they can now focus on growth.

It's in that growth that the real excitement of owning a business begins. Once an entrepreneur knows what tomorrow will bring and that tomorrow will be the same as today, the business starts to lose interest. The attraction of entrepreneurship is the endless possibilities, the not-knowing whether you're building something that will become a giant corporation, deliver a giant buyout check or just fizzle and die. Every day as an entrepreneur is another roll of the dice, another tick on the lottery ticket. Once the company is stable but no longer growing, the lottery is over. The game is run and it quickly becomes time to start thinking about the next project.

The challenge then is when and how to call it a day. Yet, it's not the biggest challenge an entrepreneur will face. Eventually, an entrepreneur will always find their way out of anything. And it's a very important quality to know this. A business that has revenues and can pay its bills will always be attractive to someone. An entrepreneur might sell the firm to another entrepreneur or possibly to one of their staff, but eventually, even if they're not forced to close a business, an entrepreneur knows when to call a project complete.

Most business projects have clear endings. They end with a dramatic offer or more commonly, a realization that it's not going to work. But entrepreneurs keep going until the end, and only they can decide when that end comes.

30

You Don't Believe In Real Life

The most amazing thing about being an entrepreneur is seeing an idea that you envisioned become real. Whether you had thought of a product that people can hold and use, an app that they can be installed on their phones or a chain of restaurants serving organic food from Burkina Faso, you had the idea and that idea was just a concept in your head.

Through hard work you make that idea real. You make it physical. You make it happen.

However, it only happens if you're prepared to focus on the vision and ignore the real world, at least initially.

No one capable of assessing risk rationally would agree to put in the kind of hours required to make a new business work when the chances of success are so small. Entrepreneurs have to be like the 80 percent of drivers who rate their driving skills as above average. That tendency, which psychologists call "illusory superiority" affects other aspects of life. In one classic study, 94 percent of university professors who took part believed that they were above average in comparison to their peers.

Every entrepreneur opens their business with the belief that they're not like all of the other entrepreneurs whose companies have collapsed and died. They're better equipped. Their idea is better. They have more drive. They have something that all of those other people who tried and failed didn't have even though they too may have something that collapses and dies, they thought they had what it took to make this one work and that they could do it.

Entrepreneurs might tell themselves that most businesses fail within a couple of years (or weeks or minutes or whatever the duration was on the last business blog they read) but those kind of real world facts don't apply to people like them.

And, they'd be right because not only do entrepreneurs overrate their own chances of success, they also underestimate other people's chances. When StatisticBrain.com, a website that collects data across different sources, examined the survival rates of businesses in different industries, it found that 58 percent of new businesses in finance, insurance or real estate were still operating after four years. More than half of companies in agriculture, services, wholesale and mining were also still going. Across all industry sectors, only a quarter of new businesses failed in their first year and nearly two-thirds made it into year three.

Whether entrepreneurs believe that most businesses collapse almost as soon as they're founded or whether they know that they actually have a one-in-four chance of running that business for twelve months, they assume that they'll either still be leading it in ten years (when 71 percent of business have failed, according to StatisticBrain.com), or they'll have already sold it and be sipping Pina Coladas on the beach.

What actually happens in the real world doesn't matter. All that matters is that they have a vision and the desire to make that decision and vision, real.

That faith in their ability extends beyond their expected survival rate to their own abilities. And not just the depths of their talent but the broadness of their skills. Ask any successful entrepreneur what surprised them most in their rise to the top, and they'll stop and think and wonder which surprise to choose first. When entrepreneurs on MosaicHub, a site for business owners, were asked about the biggest surprise they encountered as entrepreneurs.

The answers included the amount of time it takes to gain traction; the gap between the drive of an entrepreneur and the ambition of an employee; the negotiations over control when investors come in; even the feelings of loneliness and doubt they felt when they left the workplace and started out on their own.

Entrepreneurs face surprises every week, from meetings with investors that are nothing like anything they've ever had to do before to managing employees and assessing sudden opportunities to buy up rivals or team up with partners.

In the real world, these things are hard. They're tests that no new entrepreneur has ever had to face when they were working for someone else. They might be taught in business schools but there's nothing like the challenges that the real world throws up and at you that an entrepreneur will only meet when they're running their business.

Entrepreneurs can't predict the challenges that the world will deliver to them but they have to believe that they can cope with them. The belief can only happen when they're willing to ignore that there's a real world full of tricks and troubles and traps waiting for the business they're building. But the entrepreneur truly believes and assumes that if they build it, it *will* work.

Even if entrepreneurs don't believe in the real world, they do know it's there and they know how negotiate and travel through the world and to use the real world to the benefit of their idea. Successful businesses always start in the head of an innovator, an inventor or a dreamer.

They require faith and belief to turn those ideas from a vision into an office and a product. But at some point that idea will meet the real world and all its challenges, and at that moment, an entrepreneur has to continue believing in their unrealistic chances of success while also recognizing the rules of the market and the reality that customers really do want their products.

Part 4

Process

Just as there is no one and only entrepreneurial personality so there is no one entrepreneurial process or journey. Every business-builder has to create their own game plan. Even when they're working in an industry with a well-trodden path to success and familiar techniques, no two businesses ever start in the same place, face the same challenges nor run the same way. Every entrepreneur has to find their own way over the hurdles put in front of them, and create their own tools and techniques that will allow them to forge their own path to success.

There is one thing that all entrepreneurs know and that is that the only time they actually can lose is when they stop believing and stop trying—when they listen to the other people who tell them that they can't do it (and those people are always there, and always have something to tell them).

An entrepreneur (which is you, if you've read this far) believes that a rejection is never final; instead, it is a reminder that they still have a long way to go.

They understand that they have to keep track of their competitors, and they love staying up to date with their industry news. By keeping current an entrepreneur will avoid repeating what other people have done that hasn't worked and they look for and can find their own special niche.

Entrepreneurs are flexible about the rewards they receive as they build their business; money may not always be perfect and revenues can take time to grow, but in the meantime, anything that helps to move the entrepreneur or their business forward is welcome.

They also know where "forward" leads and they're capable of juggling tasks to get themselves there. When an entrepreneur is building a business, they have to know how to drive the bulldozer while still drawing the map and negotiating the contracts. In short—they do it, maybe not perfectly, but the operative word is "do."

One of the most fascinating things about businesses, even two businesses in the same field, is how much they differ from each other. Nearly all business is built with intelligence, determination and hard work. These are the essential ingredients of every product or service building process. These are principally the indispensable components of life as well.

31

You Think "No" Means "Not Yet"

"Apologies for the delayed response. We've had a chance to discuss internally, and unfortunately don't think it's the right opportunity for ____ from an investment perspective. The potential market opportunity does not seem large enough for our required model."

"...while this sounds interesting it is not something we would do here—not in our area of focus. We do wish you best of luck"

"We decided yesterday not take this to the next level. We've always struggled with travel as a category."

I f you're ever been lucky enough to find yourself in the conference room of Union City Ventures, Fred Wilson's venture capital firm, you might be surprised to see a box of breakfast cereal on the bookshelf.

You'd be even more surprised to see that the cereal is called "Obama O's," and the box features a drawing of the President tucking into a bowl of Cheerios.

The box was designed by Brian Chesky who gave them to bloggers during the 2008 Democratic National Convention to promote his bedroom letting service. He also sold them at $40 a box at the convention itself raising $30,000. Wilson keeps that box in his conference room to remind him of what he has called his biggest mistake: rejecting Airbnb's pitch for funding.

Wilson shouldn't feel too bad. The rejection emails at the top of the page are three of the five rejections Chesky received after pitching to seven VC firms on one day in June 2008. He published the rejections on Medium. Two of the firms didn't even bother to reply. His ask? A mere $150,000 at a $1.5 million valuation.

Seven VC executives, experts at spotting entrepreneurial talent, had turned down the chance to own 10 percent of Airbnb for just $150,000. Seven years later that small investment would have been worth $2.4 billion. Fred Wilson might not own a chunk of Airbnb but he certainly owns what has to be the world's most expensive box of cereal. Wilson paid dearly for the knowledge he has gained and often entrepreneurs have to pay a heavy price.

Years ago, I listened to a man speak who was in manufacturing. He had had someone come to him and pitch an idea about Velcro for the back of a bra. He laughed. Velcro seems like it's always been here to most people, however it was discovered and built by George de Mestral who noticed that burrs kept sticking to his dogs fur when he took his dog for a walk. De Mestral's own company which was also in manufacturing laughed too, but George forged ahead and figured out how to make Velcro from looking at how the burrs he pulled out of his dogs fur, worked.

They told George to quit messing around and get back to work. But what George did was just the "quit" part. The man who was speaking about Velcro said in his speech that every time he hears that "sound of Velcro," it made him physically sick.

Entrepreneurs understand that the road to success is paved with rejection. They're going to hear "no" a thousand times before someone finally, courageously, agrees to give them the nod. It often seems like no one ever wants to be the first to say "yes" in an industry. It's much easier for someone to throw in their money after that brave someone else has written a check or placed an order than for them to take the first step.

Therefore, entrepreneurs will always hear "no," and if they're going to build anything they have to hear that "no" as a "not yet." *Possibly* this investor might not be interested in them, but maybe they will be interested later. Or, perhaps the next investor will be excited. This lead might not be willing to place a key order but there are plenty more leads out there, and one of them will say "yes."

In fact, a rejection isn't just inevitable. It just might just be desirable. Responding to a comment on a blog post defending Bitcoin, Fred Wilson argued that when VCs fail to vote to invest, it's a great sign for the company. "Zero hands in a room of VCs is the single best bullish indicator I know of," he typed. "VCs are sheep being herded by hype."

There are several reasons rejection may actually be a good sign. If VCs are saying "no" to an idea, then other entrepreneurs with a similar idea are also being put off. That means there will be less competition because the competition is being weeded out by the "no's" and a greater chance of success can present itself in the future.

An entrepreneur who hears a "no" as a "not yet" and keeps plugging forward will find that those rejectionists have culled much of the competition for them. Also, along the way of the "no" you will pick up some great ideas.

For instance, "If your product had such and such, it might be something we would be interested in." Bingo! How about, "Well I had someone in here a couple of weeks ago and they had this (marvelous) idea that was better than this." Bingo! The entrepreneur will begin to move on the "Bingo's."

It also means that the person who does eventually agree to your proposal is going to be much more committed than an average backer. If they're prepared to put in funds when other people have said "no" it's because they really love the idea. They're not going to run at the first sign of trouble, and they will be ready with advice and a close relationship. At this point you have usually found yourself a mentor.

This investor and mentor will have a motivation that goes beyond their love of the business idea or even the growth of their investment. When that idea takes off, they'll be known as the only person who saw the magic in it. They get the prestige of being the visionary who identified the talent and spotted the opportunity. That's a huge incentive.

No big business idea has ever been built without rejection, and the biggest ideas often rack up the highest numbers of rejections. Any sharing company pitching for funds can now call itself the "Airbnb of" their market niche or the "Uber of" their field.

But those groundbreaking companies had nothing to compare themselves to. They were expecting investors to take a chance with something completely new, something that had no record of success for the investors to look at. The risk was bigger, so the number of rejections would have been bigger, and the rewards have now proved to be much bigger too.

The moment that any entrepreneur starts thinking of building a business, they know they're going to be rejected. They know they're going to hear the word "no." Count on it.

They also understand that that "no" really means "not yet" and the longer they have to wait for that acceptance, the more powerful it will be when it comes.

32

You Know What
Everyone Else Is Doing

E very entrepreneur's morning routine is different. Some like to
start their day with a vegetable or protein shake and a quick run
as the sun rises. Some roll out of bed in the afternoon, land on the
game controller they were crunching all night and fall into the shower.
Most just make their commute to their offices, greet the admins and fire
up their computers.

Once they've checked their own emails, the first work action, the
first step they take in that day's business building is often to see what
other people are doing and saying.

Entrepreneurs in hi-tech log on to GitHub to see what other
developers are doing. Everyone checks LinkedIn to see what other people

in their field have posted. They browse corporate blogs and check out the Twitter streams and Facebook pages of the most important people working in their space.

When the big chances to meet in person crop up—at conferences and get-togethers like—SXSW -they block out valuable space in their calendar and make a point of talking to people who understand their business and are influencing their market.

There are a bunch of different reasons for that burning desire to know what other people are doing. Part of it is a professional requirement. Understanding what competitors are doing and saying—and how quickly they're doing it—is vital. While entrepreneurs working in competing fields won't sit down and explain all the features of their new product to their rivals, they will reveal the direction they're taking. Even companies as secretive as Apple and Samsung leak out details that get audiences excited and encourage them to hold out for their next release instead of buying now.

Entrepreneurs will always soak up every leak and rumor that relates to their field—and they know enough to reject the wildest stories.

They have to know if a rival firm is working on adding a new feature to their product. They need to know when the competition is planning to launch. And they have to know which direction they believe the market is going to go.

That need for knowledge extends beyond the activities of competitors to the work of potential partners. The owner of a business creating a new plugin for WordPress, for example, will want to keep track of the work of WordPress theme designers and the developers of other plugins to look for synergies and the chance to cross-market.

If watchmakers hadn't been following Apple's move towards the iWatch they would have missed an opportunity to compete in a market that the giant tech company was opening for them.

It has been said that no product is ever born in isolation and that no business is an island. Entrepreneurs have to know what's happening in the world around them if they're going to understand how they fit into that world.

However, it would be wrong to say that the biggest motivation for entrepreneurs keeping track of other people in their field is a business need. Far more powerful is curiosity.

Curiosity first got them thinking about their own product. It was curiosity that made them look at someone else's product, spot the weakness and wonder what it would take to fix that soft spot. It was curiosity that gave them the special knowledge that every entrepreneur needs to create a new product.

Entrepreneurs are, by nature, nosy. They always want to know what other people are doing, even when those people are working in a completely different field. Passengers who find themselves sitting next to the owner of a business on a flight can expect to be grilled about their lives and their work and the way they do their work. All the time, even when they're not "on duty," entrepreneurs are soaking up information… and assessing it for an opportunity that other people have missed.

But, there's one more reason that entrepreneurs rush to social platforms in the morning and keep track of what's happening in their field: passion.

Once an entrepreneur commits to a project, it fills their lives. From the moment they start to the moment the business dies, sells or can run by itself, that project is the focus of their attention. That includes everything that might affect that project, from the start of the market to everyone working in it.

Before a doctoral candidate completes their thesis, they have to read every book written on their topic. They have to read all the people who wrote about it in the past, and they have to know what all the people who are working in the same field have written and are working on.

They have to be experts. They might not be the only experts but they have to be among that small group of people who have a complete grip of their topic.

Creating a business is like starting a PhD. It's going to take just as long. It's going to be even harder work. Raising funds is going to be no easier. The chances of success are even lower. And it requires just as much knowledge. Entrepreneurs check GitHub and LinkedIn and Twitter and industry blogs every day because they have to. They also do it because they want to. And they love the fact that other entrepreneurs are keeping tabs on them too.

33

You Accept Money— And Other Items Of Value

E ntrepreneurs are usually looking for one result from their work: they want money. They expect to create a product or service, sell it and put cash in their bank accounts. The success of a business can always be measured by the bottom line.

However, those numbers don't have to take the form of dollars and cents. More than 100,000 retailers now accept Bitcoin, a digital currency that operates without a national central bank. For companies selling online, taking that virtual cash can bring a few advantages.

Transactions are usually cheaper than they are for credit and debit cards. Like cash, they don't require the sharing of personal information. The transactions usually take place quickly and merchants can't be hit by chargebacks that can affect retailers who accept credit cards.

Sometimes, though, a business will accept more than the money that passes through a credit card and even more than a digital currency that isn't controlled by any country. Entrepreneurs are often willing to take *anything* of value. That might be game tickets, a new phone or a few nights in a hotel. When Jack Gallaway, president of the Tropicana hotel in Vegas, wanted to persuade the hotel owners at Ramada to invest in an expansion, he made a deal with a Phoenix-based real estate developer.

In return for a set of concept drawings and an architectural model that he could present to his company, he gave the firm a week of rooms and transportation. (His choice of developer wasn't coincidental. Ramada's chairman had worked with them before, making it harder for him to say no.) Gallaway got a free proposal. The development firm received a week's stay in a hotel. And the hotel ended up getting the expansion that Gallaway wanted.

That kind of bartering is the most common form that entrepreneurs use to offer a product or a service with real value in return for something of value that isn't money. It usually happens in a couple of different ways.

The best, and most frequent, time when businesses are open to barter is when they're just starting up. They have plenty of immediate needs but little cash. So they agree to do a Web design in return for a few months of hosting. Or they give away a product to an accountant in return for doing their tax returns.

However, it may be the worst time to pay with a service instead of cash. The business is in a weak state. It has little money and is desperate for services that it needs. While paying in kind is easier than dipping into scarce cash, the number of businesses willing to accept barter is smaller than the number of businesses willing to accept cash.

Restrict your choice of suppliers only to those that happen to need your service right now and are willing to take it instead of money, and you're probably going to receive lower quality service than you could have bought.

While bartering at the start of a new business looks tempting, it usually comes with a big cost.

A better time for businesses to give and take services instead of money is when they're already up and running, and when both sides know and trust each other. At that point the barter doesn't come out of need but out of respect. Each entrepreneur places a value on the other's work. They'd each want to buy from each other but instead of swapping cash, they exchange goods or services of equal value.

It's estimating that value that's difficult. Cash shows how much it's worth but a service or even a product has a different value to the person who makes it than the person who receives it. The difference is the profit and that's the real cost of the barter.

That's why entrepreneurs who engage in barter base the value of the exchange on the retail price, not the production cost. The difference is how much they're losing by giving their product away instead of selling it.

When the exchange happens regularly, instead of being a one-off, entrepreneurs also place limits on the amounts they're willing to accept or give away. Receiving free tickets to a ball game every month in return for maintaining the team's website is nice, but tickets aren't currency. They don't pay the rent and you can't use them in the grocery store. When an entrepreneur accepts a goods instead of a check, they make sure they don't do it too often and from too many different suppliers.

And, they also declare it. That's one difference between an entrepreneur and everyone else. When two friends agree to exchange favors, the agreement is no one's business but their own. When an entrepreneur receives something of value in return for something else valuable, it needs to go on their tax form. That might take some of the fun out of the exchange but it has to be done.

In practice, once an entrepreneur has a business up and running, most of their income will be in the form of cold, hard cash, which is just the way they like it. When an opportunity does arise to received something that isn't green and paper, entrepreneurs like to accept it because while money is essential, it's not the reason they create their products.

Entrepreneurs build businesses for the challenge, for the fun, for the achievement and because they can't imagine doing anything else. If someone offers them something valuable and cool in return for the work that they do, as long as it doesn't replace all their cash flow, entrepreneurs are likely to smile and grab it.

34

You Have Your Eyes On The Prize

Few people start a new business with the aim of making money. That sounds bizarre. What is a business for if not to make cash? According to a 2013 survey of small business owners by Cox Business, the overwhelming reason that small entrepreneurs chose to create their own firms wasn't to be rich, but to be their own boss. More than half of respondents cited independence as their main motivation. It was second only to the idea of creating something from the ground up. Those two answers alone were chosen by more than two-thirds of respondents. Only 8 percent of small business owners said that the idea of making more money was their main reason for starting their own company.

Considering how long it takes before a new business can start turning a profit, focusing on one of the other benefits of entrepreneurship is probably a good idea. But it's not enough. The independence and creativity might take someone with some entrepreneurial spirit out of the cubicle and into their own office but it won't keep that business growing and succeeding. Businesses don't live on the freedom of independence or the joy of creation.

They need money.

They need money to pay the bills that keep the business alive, and they need money to keep growing. That's crucial. A business that doesn't have the funds to keep investing can't grow. It can't develop and it can't move into new areas. It can't keep pushing itself and testing boundaries.

Entrepreneurs who are in it for the long haul enjoy their independence and they love the satisfaction that comes from building something by themselves. Yet, they know that the most important aspect of a business is the bottom line. At the end of the year, the company needs to have turned a profit or at least be pointing in a direction that will lead to a profit soon.

Entrepreneurs are always looking for a return on their investment.

That focus makes a real difference. Seventy percent of small businesses are sole proprietorships. They do enough business to keep the owner working. They deliver an income and they do all of things that two-thirds of small business owners wanted when they started their firms: they give them independence and they let them feel that they're building something, from scratch and with little help from others. But when those business owners don't look for a return on investment, they remain sole proprietorships. They don't grow. They replace a cubicle in an open office with a personal office in the spare bedroom. They replace a job working for someone else with a job that they can do on their own terms. They give the business owner control over their own schedule but they don't give them control over someone else's schedule or allow them to move from the spare bedroom into their own office building.

When entrepreneurs keep their eye on the prize, they do more than pay themselves a salary. And they do more than enjoy the opportunity to work for themselves. They create for themselves an opportunity to expand, and to find their own limits. They give themselves the chance to be all that they can be.

That takes work. It's not enough to look at the monthly revenues and think: "That's the rent paid and the food on the table."

Entrepreneurs who look at ROI are always thinking about ways to improve those returns. They might experiment with different pricing combinations. They might think about new product ranges. They might even take the tough decisions to lay off staff who aren't pulling their weight or being productive enough. No one ever starts their own business with the aim of culling staff members; those conversations are the worst parts of being your own boss.

But, entrepreneurs know that firing people is a necessary part of being an entrepreneur. They're prepared to hold those conversations, even though they're painful, because they know that the result will be higher returns and the growth of the company. It's one of the differences between being an entrepreneur and being a freelancer.

That difference extends to the way entrepreneurs think about their businesses. The story of Steve Jobs walking into Jonathan Ive's design department at Apple and being thrilled at what he finds is moving because we can't help but feel that the former calligraphy student might just have preferred to have spent his days in that office instead of his own. He would have loved to be have been Jonathan Ive, designing beautiful objects and enjoying the thrill of seeing his plans machined, made and used.

However, Jobs was an entrepreneur, not a designer. His focus was always on the bottom line: how much would it cost to develop a new product line? How could he mass produce it at the highest possible quality and the lowest possible price? How much could he charge for it when he was done? It meant that he was removed from a more creative role in favor of a far more important and powerful one. It also meant that Apple was able to become the world's most valuable company capable of turning luxury products at luxury prices into objects bought by millions.

Entrepreneurs might have all sorts of reasons for wanting to start their own companies. They might draw a range of different benefits from the work that they do every day. They might value their independence and feel enormous pride at what they've accomplished. But, the entrepreneurs who go on to build something spectacular always do so by understanding that it's the ROI that keeps a business alive, moving forward and creating new opportunities.

35

You Hear "Me-Too"
And Think "I'm Out"

A t a conference held in 2012, entrepreneurs and investors building medical devices came together to discuss the state of the industry. A common theme throughout the event was the lack of funding. A panel of five VC managers explained what was going on. Venture capitalists were avoiding innovative, new products and throwing their money at devices that would more readily overcome regulatory hurdles. They were all told that money was more likely to be in the products similar to devices that are already being used.

"We're flogging dead horses," Easton Capital Investment Group managing director John Friedman said in a press release issued by

Lightstone Ventures, an investment firm. "We've moved away from what's great about venture capital, which is innovation. We keep doing the same thing."

Funders, he argued, preferred to put money into projects that slightly improved existing technologies in the hope that the path to FDA approval would be easier and cheaper. The product would also be an easier buy for a larger company looking to "cover its bases."

It's a problem that's not unique to the medical industry. Any new business that tries to pitch to venture capitalists soon finds itself writing on the opening page of its Powerpoint presentation, "the Uber of..." or, "the Facebook of..." or whatever the current start-up of the month happens to be.

Investors might be paid to take risks but they still want that risk to be as small as possible. When a company offers them a venture that takes a business model that's already proven itself, it's much easier for them to both understand it and to approve it. They can see the route to growth. They can imagine the market and they know what sort of benchmarks they'll be able to use to measure success.

More importantly, if everything does go belly-up, they'll be covered. They'll be able to point to the investment of plenty of other VCs in companies that were very similar. While mistakes will always happen in VC investments, part of the consideration of the investor will always be how they will be able to explain losing the money entrusted to the company. It's easier to have an excuse ready to hand when a product is similar to one that's already succeeding.

True innovators, people who want to create something that no one has made before, will look more risky to VCs as investments. There is no way to know whether they're going to open up an entirely new market such as Oculus Rift has done for virtual reality, and enjoy a monopoly for a few years before other companies pile in behind them. Or whether people are going to react by scratching their heads and wondering what that's all about. When it's harder for investors to see the road ahead, they're less likely to give the company the fuel to drive there.

That's a problem for entrepreneurs. In fact, it presents two problems for entrepreneurs.

The first problem is that it means the road ahead is crowded. When venture capitalists are all funding similar ideas, lots of only slightly different companies are going to be competing for the same market. Eventually, the field narrows. A few big firms, strengthened by brand name recognition, cross-marketing and giant budgets, will soon dominate the field. A few smaller firms may stay within a small niche, catering to a limited market from which they'll never grow. Some of the companies may be bought up by larger firms that feel that they too should be operating in that space, but don't have the knowledge to move into it too quickly. And plenty of companies will find that they're just pushed off the road. The dotcom crash of the late nineties littered the roadside with the bodies of "me-too" companies that had burned through cash donated by risk-averse VC firms.

It's bad enough developing an unoriginal idea in a competitive environment but there's an even worse problem with building a me-too company. For a true entrepreneur, it's *not interesting*. One of the biggest thrills about creating a new business is doing something that no one has ever done before. It's the excitement that comes from dreaming up a concept then seeing it come to life.

Of course, very few ideas are ever completely original. Every company builds on what has come before. Microsoft didn't invent the computer operating system. It just built one that could work on computers in homes as well as businesses.

WiTricity didn't invent wireless charging. It's just doing it on a bigger scale than anyone had done before. Even Apple didn't invent the smartphone or the tablet computer; both had been tried before. The company just made both with enough style to make them desirable and the timing has to be right.

When the difference between what's already available is incremental rather than fundamental, when it strengthens one weakness in a rival's product instead of creating something almost completely new, the success of the product doesn't depend on the concept. It's not about the idea; it's about the process.

For a few entrepreneurs, that may be fine. They may be happy to win with a better production process in the same way that Henry Ford was content to beat competitors with a new kind of production line. But Ford's idea was big and it was as powerful as inventing a new kind of engine or a new design of car. For most entrepreneurs, the driving force that takes them from drawing board and business plan through years of development and growth is doing something that changes the world or at least the part of it in which they operate.

At the 2012 medical devices conference, John Friedman stated that he was seeing not a regression to the mean, but to mediocrity, and he warned businesses that if they see "more than five, half a dozen, a dozen companies in an area," they should move away from that area.

Occasionally, investors will describe their unwillingness to invest in more me-too companies and claim that they want to see more original ideas even as they continue to turn up their noses at innovative concepts. And entrepreneurs will continue to run from those me-too ideas and bang at the doors of investors and markets to try to change the world.

36

You Can Do Three Impossible Things At The Same Time

On April 8, 2016, SpaceX sent a rocket to the International Space Station. It was the eighth resupply mission the company had flown but it differed in two important ways. First, it delivered a new inflatable module that would expand the station; and second, after the first stage of the rocket detached itself from the rest of the vehicle, it flipped itself around and using rocket power and fins steered itself to land upright on a robotic platform in the middle of the Atlantic Ocean.

It was the second impossible thing that SpaceX's owner, Elon Musk, had done in the space of little more than a week. At the end of March, his car company Tesla had announced the launch of its Model 3 electric car. By the end of the week, the company had racked up 325,000 preorders, allowing the company to say that it had made the "biggest one-week launch of any product ever."

If doing two impossible things in a week wasn't enough, Musk also part-owns a solar company and is trying to develop a unique hyperloop between San Francisco and Los Angeles.

Few entrepreneurs have set themselves goals as ambitious as Elon Musk has done. Even fewer have achieved even one of them, let alone two in less than ten days.

All entrepreneurs have to do things that other people would find impossible. In the *Harvard Business Review*, venture capitalist and author Anthony Tjan has argued that early stage CEOs have three important tasks to complete in a business: planning, selling and executing. Each of these tasks, he contends, requires different mindsets.

For big-picture planning, entrepreneurs need to be able to develop a general idea of where they want the company to go. Without becoming too bogged down in details, they have to build a clear purpose and lay out the priorities for achieving them while still leaving room to adjust according to market research and customer feedback.

The first impossible task of an entrepreneur is to be an architect of the future, to envision a business and a product that hasn't yet been created.

The second impossible task is to share that vision with other people, and make them as excited about it as they are. They have to persuade skeptical investors that the idea in their head can become real, and that they're the only person who can make it happen. They have to generate a sense of pride among employees so that they're keen to keep building and want to keep working, not just for the money but for the sense of achievement that finishing the project successfully will bring.

They have to convince buyers that the product is the best solution to their problems that their money can buy. Even if they're not out there on the front lines, guiding shoppers to the shelves and putting the product in their hands, they have to decide on the messages that are most likely to persuade and the campaigns that will get those messages across.

Finally, impossible task number three is the execution itself, which is what makes the difference between the owner of a business and the owner of a dream. The execution is what makes the vision real, and it's the task that comes without a blueprint or a manual. Entrepreneurs simply have to be able to figure out for themselves the steps that are needed to begin building their idea.

The process will be different for every business. The challenge will be different for every project. The problems will never repeat themselves and will always require entirely new and creative solutions. Every successful business idea always starts with nothing but a notion and ends with something that people can use and touch and feel. It's an idea that ends up making people's lives better.

Every one of those tasks is impossible. They aren't like compiling lists of potential customers to upload to Salesforce or writing copy that can improve response rates. Web designers build thousands of Websites with their accompanying Webpages over their careers; being asked to produce another is part of their daily routine. They have processes they can follow and models to copy. It's doable.

What an entrepreneur does is unique. Even serial entrepreneurs, people who have built companies, sold them for sacks of cash then started another company, understand that their experience will only take them so far. No two businesses will ever be alike. No solution used to solve a problem at a previous firm will fit exactly the challenges thrown up by their next business. Each business will require its own set of rules and the entrepreneur will always have to create an entirely new plan, and sketch out a route to its construction.

They'll have to find new marketing messages, often using different processes from those they created before when they find the last ones they used don't fit. They'll have to persuade different investors to put in funds and different customers that they have a solution to a completely different problem to one they successful solved in the past. And they'll be managing a different team, steering its members towards a different goal, using different incentives and battling a different set of politics while coming to understand a different set of skills.

It's all impossible, yet entrepreneurs do it every day. They dream and plan, pitch and communicate, build and motivate. They can do all of those things in a single day, then get up and do it again the next day. And when they've done it once they'll start all over again.

Building a successful business isn't rocket science. It's more impossible than that.

37

You Do Your Homework

Every entrepreneur will have had the experience of coming up with a brilliant idea, telling it to a friend and watching their eyes glaze over. They'll wonder why their friend isn't leaping around in excitement and begging to be allowed to help make it happen. And then the entrepreneur will go away and think about it, and realize that actually their friend was right to wonder what they were talking about. The idea *was* poor, and it's lucky they figured it out now and not after they've invested a year of their life and a million dollars in it.

Every entrepreneur will also have the experience of investing at least a year of their life, and if not a million dollars, then they will spend a sizable chunk of cash, and they'll put it into an idea that their friends sort of liked but which failed anyway.

That's usually because there's only one judge of whether a business idea has legs and that's the market. Only the customer has a real vote, and only the customer will tell an entrepreneur whether their idea will live or die, solve their problem or become a problem. The customer is the true teacher for the entrepreneur.

Entrepreneurs do their homework. They trust their gut but they believe in research. They collect the survey data, run the tests and gather the numbers that will tell them whether their idea has a good foundation or not.

The benefits that market research brings are huge. Ask the right questions and you can find out not just whether there's a demand at all for a product like the one you want to build, but how much customers would be prepared to pay for it. Sometimes those figures can be higher than the price you might have thought you could charge and sometimes they turn out to be too low to make building the product worthwhile. Either way, it's information that's good to know before work on the product begins.

Supporting data will also take "pride of place" in any pitch to investors. It's one thing to be able to say that people are going to love this product; it's another to be able to point to real figures that prove that what you're saying is true.

Market research can throw up all sort of information that you might never have thought of, such as the best social media platform on which to engage people, or accessories customers might prefer to buy. Good market research provides vital intelligence for any business, which is why entrepreneurs don't skip this step—ever.

Primary market research has four forms. Exit surveys stop people on their way out of a store or a website to ask their opinion. On-site fieldwork gathers information about business location and how easily customers can access it. Interviews conducted in person or by telephone can reveal customers' likes, dislikes and preferences. And focus groups usually consist of between eight and 20 people who might try a product or discuss an idea while a researcher notes their responses.

All of those methods can yield valuable insight. The problem is that they're also expensive. Large firms may be able to pay survey companies to stop shoppers in supermarkets and bring focus groups into studios but they have deep pockets and large marketing budgets. Primary research may be valuable but it's also an expense that's often beyond the budget of a new company still preparing its investment pitch.

New companies usually have to depend on secondary research. These are surveys conducted by other businesses, often consultancies that want to create a snapshot of a market. They won't answer the specific questions that the entrepreneur might want to ask but they can give an impression of what the market wants.

That sort of data can often be found on the websites of industrial advocate groups, some government websites and in white papers offered by research companies. They're produced to promote the sponsor's interest but even the free surveys can produce some useful information and the reports that cost hundreds and sometimes even thousands of dollars can be worth the expense.

Doing that research is an essential stage in the development process of any new businesses. Entrepreneurs know that just because they have a great idea, it doesn't mean it's going to be profitable. They have to be certain that customers will make the purchase, and that the purchase will happen at a rate and price that makes the business worthwhile.

However, there's another aspect to market research that entrepreneurs avoid. Conducting research is always exciting. It's a fascinating time. You're learning so much about the market and the industry. You're gathering all sorts of information and gaining a detailed picture of what the business needs to do. Every report you read tells you something new. Every survey reveals more information and provides a new perspective. Every new Excel sheet of numbers can be manipulated and counted until it squeezes out more secrets, sending you running back to produce more survey questions.

For an entrepreneur passionate about their industry, as every entrepreneur has to be, market research can be addictive. Nothing else can tell you so much about your favorite subject and there's always more to know. No one report can answer every question so it always feels as though one more bit of information is needed to fill in a gap.

The risk is that all of that research comes to replace action. Instead of building, you read. Instead of hiring, you buy another report. Instead of creating a minimum viable product, you opt for another massive spreadsheet. This is a well known psychological phenomenon. It is what happens when you are afraid. When the risk is really big. When you are procrastinating.

Entrepreneurs know that they have to perform market research before they start work on their project. But they also know when the research has to stop and the work has to begin. And they do it.

Part 5

Goals

In theory, every entrepreneur should have the same goal: to be rich. To anyone who *isn't* an entrepreneur that certainly looks like the ideal destination. All successful business leaders are rewarded with giant sacks of cash. Their stock options enable them to buy large houses, vacation homes and expensive cars or whatever the entrepreneur happens to be into, at least this is what it often looks like to someone looking in at a successful person.

While the life of a successful entrepreneur might include luxuries, they aren't the main benefits of an entrepreneurial life. Employees, too, can take vacations in beautiful locations. Not everyone who drives a Porsche or a Tesla has founded a business sold to Google, and big houses might be grand, but if you're in the office for a dozen hours a day and on the road for several days a month, a smaller home might be a better consolation for knocking off at five and quiet weekends every week with the family.

Entrepreneurs have lots of stuff but they rarely have lots of time so if the goal of business-building was all about wealth, many of the most successful entrepreneurs would actually be among the world's biggest failures.

In fact, the goals and motivations of an entrepreneur are usually both simpler and more difficult to understand.

Entrepreneurs want to change the world. They want to build their dreams. And, they want to win.

38

You Want To Shake Things Up

What has BMW done lately? It's launched new models, some of which have some radically new features. Of course, the BMWi8 with the tiny turbocharged three-cylinder engine that drive the rear wheels. The i3 is all-electric. The company's Active Assist brings completely autonomous cars a step closer.

Both of those moves are dramatic and in both of them the automotive giant is following, not leading. Tesla, a company created thirteen years before BMW's centenary, remains the leader in electric cars. Google, a business dependent on Internet searches, has been setting the standard for cars that can drive themselves.

That's not unusual. When a large company has been doing something well and successfully for a long time, it becomes conservative. It's hit on a formula that works, so why change it? If you have a product or a service that's doing well, why risk it all on something new?

When you're winning at one game, why switch? To expect a company the size of BMW to change the way people drive their cars and create an entirely new automotive market is like expecting Novak Djokovic to walk out on the tennis court with a double-ended tennis racquet with two square heads. He knows the rules and he's mastered them. What could he gain by changing them?

Therefore, the changes that come from big companies tend to be incremental. Under pressure from legislators, car engines become a little greener. In response to competition, they become a little more powerful. After seeing sales of SUVs rise, companies tell their designers to make their cars a little bigger. Overall, little changes.

The cars on the road today may be faster, more comfortable, easier to drive and better built than those that rolled off Ford's conveyor belts at the start of the last century but the fundamentals are the same. And, the logos on the front of those will have changed very little too. All of the major automakers are venerable, old firms that benefit from doing roughly the same thing that they've always done.

Whatever revolutionary spirit had once brought them into the industry has gone the same way as the company's founder. The boards that run those firms now are made up of people who led companies rather than people who created them. BMW's supervisory board is led by engineers who worked their way to senior positions in the company, not entrepreneurs who built other businesses.

It takes an entrepreneur to make big changes, to look at a situation that benefits a few giant players and to see an opportunity for a nimble newcomer. It takes the vision of an entrepreneur to spot that chance, and the courage and confidence of an entrepreneur to act on it. It's a tough move to make. Those large companies will have grown rich in an unchanging industry. They'll have the networks, the connections, the infrastructure and the marketing budget to keep competitors out. If a competitor looks like it might make break through, they also have the cash to buy them up and kill them off.

Microsoft grew quickly by changing the way that people used computers but it stayed big by using its position to stop other competitors from installing their own software. Bill Gates had the innovation of an entrepreneur but once his company dominated its field, he made sure that field didn't change. That's how big companies stay big.

Mark Zuckerberg is doing both. On the one hand, whenever a social media company looks like it could take market share with a rival service, he acts quickly to try to stifle it. He saw that video content would be more important than text so offered $3 billion for Snapchat, a video content service with no revenues. Evan Spiegel, Snapchat's founder, is an entrepreneur from head to toe. He turned down a sum of money that could have enabled him to live a life of luxury in favor of the chance to create change. He's determined to continue building his service and to change the way that people communicate. Facebook has since launched a rival service. Whichever side wins, Spiegel will have made a difference.

At the same time, though, we can see Zuckerberg's entrepreneurial spirit in his leadership of virtual reality. He managed to buy Oculus Rift, a Two Billion acquisition that left many observers scratching their heads. While Zuckerberg wants to keep Facebook at the top of social media, he's happy to keep changing the way in which people consume the content that's shared through that media.

He sees virtual reality as the future and he's now using all the power that Facebook has gathered to make that happen. Because it's a direction that complements, rather than competes with a way of doing things that has already brought success, he can keep pushing and keep changing up the Facebook scene. Now, Zuck has reached in and snagged Snapchat, in Oct 2016 for a cool Five Billion. He's got a plan and he is keeping his sight on his goals.

For people who have worked their way up through companies to the corner office, the world has been good to them. They studied well, worked hard and won the rewards that they deserved. They're proof that the status quo works—so there's no need to change it. However, that business model in itself is beginning to change and has a much smaller chance of survival than it used to.

An entrepreneur comes from outside the status quo. To break into an industry, they're going to have to smash walls and defeat defenders. They'll have to be creative and they're not afraid to smash and burn everything that gets in their way or holds them back. In fact, that's part of the fun.

The real challenge comes after the battle, when they've finished questioning the way things have always been done, and they take action and make things better. What does an entrepreneur do when they're successful and they hear another entrepreneur knocking on their walls? They don't sit there, that's for sure. They innovate, innovate, innovate, iterate, pivot, and they do what they have to win.

39

You Live For The Dream

t took Shopify three years, which is thirty-six months after Tobias
Lütke and his co-founders launched a site to help merchants create
online stores, until they saw their first positive cash flow. They financed
those three years by taking money from angel investors, applying for
grants from the Canadian government and by not taking their own
salaries as founders.

A business can continue doing that as long as investors and others
are willing to put in money and as long as the founders are willing to put
off the moment they need to buy a new car or eat something other than
noodles, take-outs and breakfast cereal.

One rule of thumb is that in a business's first year, the founder will
earn less (and often much less) than he or she made as a salary in their

previous year. Any revenues will go straight back into the business to pay for expansion. In their second year, if they're lucky, they'll make the same money that they made with more security a couple of years earlier. If all goes well, the third year will be the first in which the business owner feels they're moving ahead, that they have more income than they used to earn and shares in an increasingly valuable company.

The timetable of success will vary from business to business. The goal of any new company is always to replace income from investors and grants with income from revenue. It's the only way to create sustainability. The length of time a business can survive until it reaches that moment will depend on the amount of money investors are willing to come up with, and how long they and other senior staff are prepared to wait to see the rewards of their risk-taking.

So, what do entrepreneurs live on while they're waiting for their businesses to become a profit?

They get by on a couple of things. They live on the cheapest, quickest food they can buy and prepare so that they don't waste cash on groceries, don't waste time cooking when they could be crunching database figures and don't keel over from hunger. This period of a company's development is called "ramen profitability" for a reason.

It's a time when the business is generating just enough money to give its founders a minimal standard of living without having to resort to a day job or a second job and a time that ends with entrepreneurs swearing that they'll never eat another bowl of ramen noodles again. It's a step up from the time when entrepreneurs are working on their company in their spare time, but it's still a step away from the moment they can feel they have achieved success. It's a tough time, but an entrepreneur hangs on.

Entrepreneurs will live on something else, too—something much more powerful and far more nutritious than a bowl of noodles: they'll live on their passion, their excitement, and their drive.

Every entrepreneurial idea starts with a spark. Sometimes, when the idea is weak, that spark dies out but occasionally it catches. It grows, it flames and it turns into a burning desire. From the moment, they realize that this is an idea that can really grow, an entrepreneur is hooked and consumed by the project they're working on. They know that they won't be able to see the result today. They know that it might be years before they get to hold their product, let alone bring in their first customers, but they also know that this is their big chance, this is the concept that will allow them to make a difference. They know this project is worth paying for in the short term.

The problem comes when passion clouds judgment. Desire is no replacement for ability and enthusiasm isn't an alternative to a cool assessment of risks. The size of a business's success isn't proportional to the degree of passion its founders feel when they started it and still felt a year after they launched it. That success depends on developing a clear vision and making smart decisions, neither of which have anything to do with passion.

One of the dangers of living on passion is that it blinds the entrepreneur to problems that the business encounters, and every business will encounter problems. It's too tempting to believe that an idea this good can't fail when the company is clearly heading straight for the ground (and someone else with the same idea is making their version fly.)

Watch Shark Tank on TV for some really good advice and some really good perspective. Some of the perspective will come to the entrepreneur themselves as they watch some of the goofballs hang onto something really really pathetic—and the person has so much drive and passion, they WILL NOT believe it when they are told that the idea is awful. An entrepreneur has to be able to wade through all of the advice, but they still need to wade.

Passion has to be strong enough to see you through those months and even years when earnings are minimal. It has to pack enough electricity to let you feel the end result when you're still years away from making it happen. It has to be the thing that sustains you when the money is tight and time to spend with friends and family is even tighter. It's the thing that makes you feel a million dollars when anyone looking from the outside will wonder what on earth you think you're doing and how long you think you're going to be doing it for. Passion isn't all you need to take you where you want to go, but is it *essential* to get you where want to go.

There are periods in every entrepreneur's life when they have to spend an excessive amount of time, building and planning and preparing, and barely make enough money to buy a morning latte. At those times it's passion that keeps them going, and it's passion packed into skill and perseverance that will see them through.

40

You Want To Win But
You're Not Afraid To Lose

At the age of 40, Bill McCloskey was working in sales for SoftImage, makers of the 3D animation software used in movies like Jurassic Park. Myst was the video game of the moment and for the first time, critics were starting to see the video game industry as a rival, or a partner, to Hollywood.

Writing on his website OnlyInfluencers.com, a community for email marketers, McCloskey explained how he developed a passion for the new industry. "I became obsessed with these games. Now THIS was something I could see myself doing," he said. He memorized the names of everyone who had helped to produce his favorite games and began thinking about his own game idea. "Dreamland" would be based on Dante's Inferno and would be heavy on storyline and script.

His work in the 3D industry introduced him to many of the developers he needed to meet. Chance brought him contacts in Hollywood. A knack for pitching brought agreements from talented people to work with him. Venture capitalists agreed to pay him half a salary, not realizing that that half-salary was more than his full salary at the time, and, in 1994, he closed a development deal with Microsoft. McCloskey quit his job and prepared to start building his dream project for his own business.

And, then it all went wrong. Steven Spielberg, David Geffen and Jeffrey Katzenberg formed Dreamworks which started working with Microsoft, but only on the condition that the software firm shut down its own game division. The Christmas video game sales figures were released, and they were terrible. Investors closed their wallets. The money run out, and by the end of 1995 McCloskey found himself jobless, penniless, with two children under six and a wife who had just been diagnosed with cancer.

It was about as deep and as low as anyone could ever be—and hope to avoid. But he got through it. His wife recovered. He set up eDataSource, now a successful service provider for email marketers, and McCloskey's a regular contributor to Reddit, helping other entrepreneurs to learn from his mistakes.

Bring together any group of successful entrepreneurs, and you'll hear a ton of stories about business-building, motivation and money-raising. You'll hear wonderful advice about finding customers and achieving goals. It will be valuable stuff that can help any entrepreneur to make their mark.

If you really want to hear great stories—the kind that make you think and think again—ask a successful entrepreneur—not about their successes—but about their failures because no entrepreneur ever succeeds the first time out. Or, if their first business does take off, it's usually their second or third or fourth that makes their name memorable. It's the challenges that reveal the opportunities, and the failures that provide the lessons that allow them to do better next time.

Entrepreneurs know that failure is inevitable. They want to win, they *have* to win, but they know that they must lose before they achieve a final victory. Just as every new athlete has to race competitors who are better than they are, and competitors who will beat them until they learn from the others and are strong enough to do better, the fight will be huge. Entrepreneurs will create businesses that fail to overcome competitors. And there will be times when the entrepreneur will fail to reach the finish line.

While every entrepreneur hates to lose, no successful entrepreneur is ever *afraid* to lose, or is *unwilling* to lose.

That doesn't mean that loss isn't painful. Every time a business collapses, a dream dies with it. Years of work and planning and sacrifice go the same way as investors' money and the kind of emotional investment that only a founder can provide.

Failure though is rarely sudden. It usually becomes clear months or even years before a final decision has to be taken. Customers fall away, profits drift downwards, competitors start eating your lunch or investors become reluctant to open their wallets. Businesses usually die slowly, which gives entrepreneurs enough time to come to terms with the end and either make adjustments or decide to end the pain quickly.

There's always a period between the beginning of trouble and the start of the end when you can see that things aren't going to work this time. That doesn't just give you time to come to terms with this defeat. It's also an opportunity to start thinking of alternatives. Because that's what entrepreneurs do. They might work on one big idea at a time (unless they're Elon Musk) but they've always got other ideas—Plans B, C, D and E—tucked away for safekeeping.

As soon as an entrepreneur can see that Plan A isn't working those new ideas start to come forward. Because there is more to bring to the table in knowledge this time, to those ideas can be added the lessons learned trying to create Plan A, and the entrepreneur will go into that venture stronger, smarter and with a better chance of success.

Being an entrepreneur means living with a competitive nature. It means hating to lose when other people can shrug and walk away. It means living with a drive to come first and an inability to accept second place. But it also means accepting that second place is a short step from first place and the only way to reach success is one step at a time.

Part 6

Lifestyle

The result of an entrepreneur's hard work should be a change in their lifestyle. Or, not. Warren Buffett famously continues to live in the same house in Omaha, Nebraska that he bought in 1958 for $31,500. Today that property is worth about $260,000. That's a pretty small buy for someone said to be worth about $39 billion.

Not every entrepreneur is so modest. Richard Branson has his own private Caribbean island which he uses for business retreats as well as for family vacations far from prying eyes. The lifestyle that an entrepreneur might choose to live once they've achieved their primary goal of building the business they want will depend on their tastes and their own personal style. But the ways that entrepreneurs live as they're building their businesses tend to have much in common.

Today's business-builders tend to have a similar, simple dress-code, especially those working in the field that made the black turtleneck and the orange t-shirt, and the grey hoodie part of the entrepreneurial uniform. They work during holidays because that's the best and quietest time to get stuff done. They know the jargon of business as well as their industry, and they size up every location, from cafés to bedrooms on the basis of their ability to deliver focus, as well as electricity and a fast wifi connection.

They might not sleep as much as they should, or at the same time that everyone else does, but they've found their own tools for getting things done quickly and efficiently, and they know the value of time… and that value is not something that can be measured in money.

Above all, their lifestyle is filled with activity. Entrepreneurs, more than anything else, make things happen because they're busy.

41

Your Suit Is A T-Shirt And
Your Favorite Label Is A Logo

I n January 2016, as Mark Zuckerberg returned to work on his first day after paternity leave, he posted a picture of his first difficult decision. "What should I wear?" he wrote under a photo of his closet. It contained nine identical grey t-shirts and eight identical and slightly darker grey hoodies.

Which color t-shirt to pull on might not be the most difficult decision Facebook's founder has to face in the office but turn the clock back a few years, and the wardrobe of a chief executive of any firm, let alone a company worth more than $325 billion, would have looked very different: tailored suits, starched shirts, fraternity cufflinks and a rack of ties as long as a couple of arms. It wasn't just the furniture and the attitudes towards women that made TV's *Mad Men* look like another world; it was the sharp suits that every man wore even when they were relaxing on the weekend.

Those days are long gone. Bankers and lawyers might still have to do up their top buttons and remember how to tie a Windsor knot but people who run their own businesses get to make their own rules. Ditching the jacket and tie isn't just a way to be more comfortable. It's a means of declaring that the wearer is the boss. No one tells them how to dress, and everyone else has to change to suit *their* relaxed style.

You can blame (or thank) Steve Jobs. It was his trademark turtlenecks that set the formula for chief executives who create the environments in which they work. But Jobs didn't always wear a black sweater and blue jeans. Look hard enough through the pictures of Jobs on Google and you can find a few images of him in shirts and suits, and even a bow tie. That two-piece outfit might have started as a comfortable choice but once it became a part of his personal brand, Jobs stuck with it. Who knows? Maybe he didn't even like it, but it was "brandable."

Everyone else has followed. Today, the uniform of the entrepreneurial geek is often the t-shirt and hoodie, and anyone who wears anything else in Silicon Valley gets as many strange looks as Lady Gaga would receive on the floor of the New York Stock Exchange. That's not to say this will not change. And, if it changes, so will everyone else.

When an entrepreneur opens their closet today, they might not find a pile of identical grey t-shirts, but they are likely to find a stack of other t-shirts. Some of them will have been picked up at festivals like SXSW. Others will display their company's name or logo. And some, no doubt, will show the names or logos of previous companies that they've created. The uniform of today's entrepreneur is a combination of business card, networking contacts, and résumé.

But, those t-shirts and jeans are still part of a uniform. They're what entrepreneurs are expected to wear as they build their businesses. They're clothes that cost little to buy, take no time to choose and they're easy to work in. But what happens when an entrepreneur reaches a point at which they no longer need to work?

Some entrepreneurs keep going. Neither Larry Page nor Sergei Brin had a particular style when they were building Google, and now that they're less involved in the day-to-day running of the business that hasn't changed. However, Jack Dorsey has become known for developing a new taste in designer suits (as well as hipster facial hair) and Elon Musk makes the style pages of fashion magazines. A profile in *Vogue* described his black t-shirt and jeans, and compared him to Tony Stark in *Iron Man*. (Robert Downey Jr. met with Musk to discuss the role, and the billionaire had a cameo in the film. His factory was even used as the villain's den in *Iron Man 2*.) Whatever Musk might have worn when he was helping to build PayPal, his first successful business, today's he's a snappy dresser who's not afraid to splash out on clothes, or wear the same thing. "Whatever," seems to be what he's saying.

If that makes him different to most entrepreneurs it's because he's gone beyond most entrepreneurs. He's already built a successful business. He's already made his fortune. He doesn't need to make any more money and his prime motivation now is changing the world for the better: ending reliance on fossil fuels; colonizing space. The burning desire that he might have felt at the start of his entrepreneurial journey has been replaced by the feeling of responsibility that comes when you have money, time and the ability to make change happen.

Even Mark Zuckerberg may not be there yet. He's still working on the business that he started in college which is why still dresses as though he hasn't left college. If entrepreneurialism has a uniform it's because that first business is really a kind of school where entrepreneurs learn how to turn an idea into product, and a product into sales.

Entrepreneurs might be happy to wear clothes that require little thought and that fit the appearance demanded of them, but once they've achieved success and graduated to the next stage of life, they can wear anything they want. In recent years we have even seen Zuckerberg wearing a suit, though usually blue or gray like the t-shirt color. It is nice to know that even Zuckerberg can wear a suit if he wants to. It really isn't dictated to him, but he knows when to be classy and he knows which outfit is classy for which day—the suit, or the t-shirt –or, *the t-shirt with the suit.* But you get what we mean.

As an entrepreneur, you have to distinguish between which outfit is classy for which day. If fashion dictates that the new VC hates all t-shirt wearers on sight, often this can be taken as a clue that you might want to wear something else. An entrepreneur knows that it is wise to (at least) have a choice already in the closet before the situation demands something different that their usual.

42

You Love Holidays Because You Can Finally Get Some Work Done

I n an interview with the *Paris Review*, author Julian Barnes described his working life. "I work seven days a week," he said. "I don't think in terms of normal office hours or rather, normal office hours for me include the weekends. Weekends are a good working time because people think you've gone away and don't disturb you. So is Christmas. Everyone's out shopping and no one phones. I always work on Christmas morning—it's a ritual."

That's a 365-day routine with which entrepreneurs can easily identify. (His writing hours of ten in the morning until one in the afternoon which are followed by revising and bill-paying look a lot easier.) For entrepreneurs, as for authors, the best times to work are the times when everyone else isn't. Fewer emails are sent so there are fewer to reply to, and any messages that do need sending can wait until after the holiday ends. They're only going to receive an "out of office" reply anyway. The atmosphere is calm and quiet. There's even less traffic on the road so for a few hours and perhaps even a few days, the pressure is off. This is "bonus work time," extra hours that let you catch up, clear the decks and even move ahead.

Entrepreneurs might not have bosses to hand them a little extra in their Christmas paychecks but they can assign themselves the opportunity for some extra achievement. They can use that quiet time to move forward with their mock-up, plan out their next A/B test or work a little more on their pitch. Even finding more research can be a useful way to fill a Thanksgiving morning while everyone else is cooking the bird or packing the car. There's a real thrill in knowing that you're sneaking ahead while the competition is snoozing in bed.

More often though, entrepreneurs have little choice. More than three-quarters of businesses have one owner and no employees so if orders aren't processed for a day or the other tasks managed, they either don't get done or they build up until the holiday ends. Either way the business suffers. For an entrepreneur, taking a vacation is unthinkable, and taking a vacation without packing their laptop is unimaginable. Christmas, Thanksgiving and other holidays have little meaning for entrepreneurs because business is now international and the Internet never stops. When a business is growing it's hard enough to keep up, let alone get ahead of it and you certainly don't want to fall behind.

This isn't just a problem for entrepreneurs though. The United States is the only industrialized country without statutory paid days off for public holidays and vacations. While workers in Britain know that they'll be getting paid for 28 days each year on which they do no work, and French employees can do nothing but drink coffees and eat croissants for 36 days each year without losing income, businesses in the U.S. don't have to give their staff any money at all if they don't work. In practice, most companies give ten days of paid vacation after the first year of employment plus another eight days of holidays. That's still half the beach and family time the French get to enjoy... and people don't take it.

According to the U.S. Travel Association, American workers leave five paid days off unclaimed each year. In effect, on those days, they're working for free. They could have stayed at home and binge-watched *Game of Thrones* all day and they would still have been paid.

The reasons that employees give for working on their days off vary. Some prefer to build up days for themselves so that they can take a longer break altogether, later. Others prefer to use the days as extra sick days or to keep some time on hand if they need to stay at home with their children or if the kids get sick. For many people, there's just too much work to do to take all the time off that they're entitled to take. When you're working for a start-up and the launch is six months away, even if you don't own the company, you want to be there for every part of that process.

That's great for the business and even better for the business owner but it doesn't do much for the employee. That's one of the big advantages of being an entrepreneur. When you own your own business, you work more hours than everyone else. There are no office hours, only time when you can grow your business and time when you have to eat, sleep and take the kids to school. You'll put in more time than the hardest-pressed employee and you'll never go 24 hours without sitting in front of your computer. The times when other people feel they can slack off a little are the best times for you to get ahead of the game and catch up on all the tasks you've put off until you had a spare moment.

When you own your own business, you get out of it exactly what you put in. The more you work, the fewer days off you take, the more holidays you ignore, the faster your business will grow and the sooner you'll reach that stage you most want to reach: the time when the business is built, and you can either sell it on or let someone else handle some of the day-to-day management. That's the day when all those missed holidays come back and every day becomes a holiday.

43

You Work More Hours Than A Doctor And Earn Less Per Hour Than A Burger Flipper

The moment when a born entrepreneur leaves their employer's office for the last time, determined to start their own business, should feel like gold. Whether the move is forced (because entrepreneurs can struggle with the limits of working for someone else) or whether it's a brave choice that just had to be made, it's a step-up, a step forward, a move in the direction that suits them more than any other.

Yet, in some ways, it's also a step down. Businesses take time to grow and earn, and until that happens the entrepreneur is going to earn less than they made in their previous job. The first goal will be to increase their earnings as quickly as possible.

And, the first way that happens is by working more hours.

Three-quarters of doctors work more than 40 hours a week and ten percent put in more than 71 hours. Lawyers too are known for their long dedication to work. Like doctors, they average 50 hours a week but between a quarter and a third, depending on the type of law firm, spend more than 60 hours a week in the office.

But both doctors and lawyers are well-paid or they know they will be once they've put in those first years and paid off their student loans. Entrepreneurs can't be that confident, and while working longer might bring closer the moment they break through, until that happens there's little relationship between the number of hours they put in and the amount of money they can take out.

The result is that once a new entrepreneur counts the money they've earned at the end of the month and divides it by the number of hours they'll have put in to make that money, they're likely to find something shocking. (Usually, it's better not to look.) Not only is the entrepreneur working harder than their friends who are lawyers or doctors but they're also earning less per hour than their teenage children who are working in Burger King or waiting tables.

It's a stunning discovery and it hits every entrepreneur at some point in the months after starting their own business, and it produces one of two responses.

Some entrepreneurs do the math, understand that this can't continue and start looking for a job. They can't see the light at the end of the tunnel, aren't sure that the tunnel will ever end and they give up. They dust off their résumés and swap long hours for a little immediate reward for slightly shorter hours with a limited reward.

Other entrepreneurs, though, double down. There's a limit to the number of hours that can be squeezed into a day, and a limit to the number of days they can squeeze into a week. So they look for ways to squeeze more work out of each hour. They follow productivity routines, improve their organization, rent an office to reduce distractions, and discover the value of outsourcing as a way of focusing on their most important tasks. They become more efficient.

Having improved their own workflow, they look at the value of the work they're producing. Even if one marketing stream is already working, they look for ways to add more, and to improve the ROI of the streams they're using. They get better at A/B testing. They read more advice about copywriting, sign up for webinars and experiment with new channels. They work smarter.

The improvement won't be immediate, but it happens. Gradually at first they start to see little tick-ups in traffic flows to websites, clicks on landing pages, and a rise in the number of email subscribers. Sales begin to increase, barely noticeably at first, but after a month or two or three, the amount of money earned per month divided by the number of hours worked each month hits the minimum wage.

Then the money starts to rise. As the marketing channels become more efficient, the sales continue to grow. As the sales funnels become more complex and the upsell and downsell offers become more attractive, the entrepreneur is able to squeeze more money out of each visitor. Each launch yields more information about the market that makes the next launch better. Each workshop and conference produces not just more knowledge but a richer selection of partners and affiliates who can increase sales.

It happens. It usually happens slowly but for the determined and the brave, it happens. Those long low paying hours at the start of a new business start to pay off. Once that hourly incomes barrier begins pushing past the bigger flipper and starts to approach the entrepreneur's old salary, which might be a year or two or even longer after they started, the entrepreneur can start cutting back on hours. They feel more confident about outsourcing a few more tasks. They have the funds to hire more people. And they understand that the more they pay for better qualified help, the higher the value of the final product and the bigger their returns.

Eventually, if they persevere, they find that they're earning more than a doctor or a lawyer and working far fewer hours, doing work that's much easier and much more enjoyable, (at least to them) and a money increase which has no limits on the amount they can earn.

Every entrepreneur knows that the life of a business-owner can be terrific. It's full of freedom and satisfaction and achievement. But, they have to pay the price for this victory, and their dues have to be paid first, at the beginning when the hours are long and the income streams are narrow and slow.

Entrepreneurs do work crazy hours and they can earn sums that would make a burger-flipper drop their patties. But, they have no limits, and for an entrepreneur, that early investment is the foundation of the business they have to build. I think every minute, hour, and year that I've dedicated to starting my businesses were well worth my life's investment of money, time, and myself.

44

You Only Speak
One Language: Business

Immigrants in the United States make up about 13 percent of the population. They're also responsible for starting more than a quarter of new businesses that open every year. As many as 40 percent of America's largest businesses, from Colgate to Kohl's and from Google to Proctor and Gamble were founded by immigrants or their children.

Those founders will have spoken all the languages of the UN: English certainly, but also German and Spanish and Russian and French and Hindi and everything in between. But whatever the first or second language of those founders, all entrepreneurs have one language that they all speak: they speak the language of business.

It's something that happens pretty quickly. Words change their meaning. When an entrepreneur hears the word "pitch" they see a room full of venture capitalists instead of twenty-two soccer players chasing a ball. When someone introduces them to their "partner," they wonder why they've brought an affiliate to a party before remembering that some people actually have love lives. And when their daughter says she wants a "unicorn," for her birthday, an entrepreneur will tell her that they're working on it, before realizing the child meant a horned horse, not a billion-dollar start-up.

It's an obsession that extends beyond business into every aspect of an entrepreneur's life. When an entrepreneur starts up a conversation with someone on a plane, there's always a hope that this new contact will be a major buyer, a potential partner who can open an entirely new market or a future employee who can crack the puzzle that's been holding the business back.

They hope at the bare minimum that this new contact will *know* something that can be used by the entrepreneur to build a better something in their business. While other people see a shake of a hand and as a friendly way to make someone's acquaintance, for an entrepreneur it's like pulling the arm of a fruit machine and hoping they'll hit the jackpot. They never know where that first conversation will lead and they're always hoping it's going to lead somewhere that helps their business.

The same is true of developments in the news. Whatever the lead story in newspapers and on news websites, the first question that pops into the mind of an entrepreneur is: "What does this mean for my company?" Entrepreneurs are always thinking about their market, their customers, the investment environment.

When a major election is coming up, they wonder what will happen to sales on election-day, to the cost of advertising when PACs are buying banners and radio spots, and to the ability to win publicity when reporters only care about the latest poll. Only after they've thought through all those issues will they remember that actually the vote will determine the future of the country and that will affect their business too.

Even technology is all about their business. Samsung releases a new phone? Entrepreneurs wonder whether it will make their phone calls more efficient or enable them to get more done while they're on the road. Smart TV gets a bit smarter? Instead of wondering whether they should buy one, entrepreneurs wonder how they can get their product on that screen.

A music company releases new sound-reducing earphones? While other people think about the clear sound they'll get when they listen to their favorite music, entrepreneurs imagine the complete silence in which they'll be able to work when they're sitting on the train or while their kids are playing at their feet.

To an entrepreneur, all those familiar terms, all the news reports that other people watch and think about and ignore, and all those products that make life more enjoyable, all have a different meaning and were made for a different purpose. They're all about their business and nothing but the business.

Entrepreneurs pick up new words too. It's not just unicorns that stop being the cast of My Little Pony. Black swans become more than attractive wild fowl; these are the unexpected events that can come as a huge surprise and have a major effect on your business and even ruin a business environment, or open a new opportunity for a savvy entrepreneur.

However, the Black swan theory is usually better seen in hindsight. Employees aren't just people who draw a salary; they have rank based on the time they joined the business and the amount of equity they have in the business. "The wild" isn't a place where bears and lions roam; it's the place to spot a new release once it's been let out of the laboratory. A sticky product isn't a phone that's been used by a kid who's just eaten a PB&J sandwich; it's one that keeps people coming back for more.

Language that used to be an easy way to communicate has become a treasury of words that have entirely different meanings to anyone not in the entrepreneur's immediate circle.

It's a form of obsession. When everything is about the business, when every event affects the company, and every new contact is assessed on their ability to improve a product or increase sales, you know that all you're thinking about is your business. When you find yourself holding an entire conversation about spotting a unicorn in the wild whose incredible hockey stick was only powerful because it was so sticky, and damn that black swan—and the people you're talking to know exactly what you're talking about, you know you're in the right company and you're all talking the same language.

Being an entrepreneur isn't just about what you do or who you are. It's about where you're going. Every entrepreneur that moves from employee to business owner is going places and they soon find themselves speaking the same language when they get there.

45

You Judge Cafés By Their Wireless And Power Outlets

New entrepreneurs don't have a commute. They don't have to battle their way through traffic to reach an office or struggle to find a parking space when they get there. But they do have a fight that's almost as tough. They have to land the best spots in the café.

Walk into any café today, from Starbucks to the local pastry shop, and you'll find digital nomads sitting at their tables, clacking away at their keyboards. For entrepreneurs, coffee shops aren't just places to load up on caffeine and croissants. They're offices where the only rent is the cost of a cappuccino.

Some cafés are better for entrepreneurs than others, and some *places* in those cafés are better than others too. When an entrepreneur walks into a café, the first thing they look for isn't the menu or the pastry window. It's the electrical outlets and the Wi-Fi password.

Electricity and Internet are the bare essentials. They're the minimum that a café needs if it's to attract and hold entrepreneurs running their own businesses, as well as the freelancers who help them. However, entrepreneurs who work in cafés should be looking at a number of other factors, too.

Security is an issue. Log on to a café's Wi-Fi network and your computer will be vulnerable to hackers. According to security firm Kaspersky, hackers can position themselves between you and the connection point, giving themselves access to every piece of information you're sending. They can also distribute malware which can let them hack into your computer any time they want.

The company recommends always browsing through a VPN when using a public network to ensure that any information sent is encrypted; enabling the option to always turn HTTPS on on websites that you visit frequently; and turning off Wi-Fi whenever you're not using it.

In practice, though, the risk from hackers is small. A bigger risk is that your screen can be seen by anyone passing behind you. A café certainly isn't a good place to check your bank account or the state of your PayPal invoices, but it also isn't a good place to work on your secret project, unless you can be certain of landing the corner spot that keeps your screen facing the wall.

Nor can you stay in a café all day. It's not an office; it's someone else's business, and if you're sitting there taking up a seat on a single cup of coffee, the owner of that business isn't making money. Cafés might be rent-free for entrepreneurs but they're not completely free. Think of a single cup of coffee as buying you a couple of hours of work, and try to avoid taking a table at lunchtime if you're not staying to eat.

Most importantly, tip well. When you're using the same café several times a week, it pays to be on good terms with the wait staff and the barista. Not only will you always get your coffee exactly the way you like it, but they'll also be more willing to turn down the music when you ask them to or tell you about the hidden electrical outlet behind the bookshelf.

The real benefit of working in a café when you're building your business though, isn't the coffee, and it isn't the chance to get out of the spare bedroom and be around people. It's the chance to interact with other people like you.

Start going to the same café every day or several times a week, and you'll come to know the other guests working in exactly the same way. They'll also be scrunched over their keyboards, checking their stats and testing their copy. Or, they'll be producing designs for their own clients or creating business plans for other entrepreneurs.

You can't go to a conference every day but going to a café every day (or every few days) can have a similar effect. You'll get to mix with other entrepreneurs, swap ideas and talk about the work that you do. You might well find that the person at the table next to you has a skill that you need to get you through the next stage, or that they're in need of the very product you're in the process of making, or that one of their friends knows the venture capitalist you were planning to email.

When cafés are filled with other entrepreneurs, they're filled with opportunity.

You can even claim further benefits. Café-working has become so popular that most major towns now have co-working centers that are places where entrepreneurs can rent a desk or even a small office. They might cost twenty or thirty dollars a day or a few hundred dollars a month for open access but they'll often include conference rooms as well as access to office facilities such as free printing and photocopying, events and workshops, and of course regular networking with other entrepreneurs building their own businesses.

One of the toughest challenges that entrepreneurs have to overcome when they make the change from an office to a spare bedroom is the realization that they're suddenly alone. There are no office politics, but also no easy chats, and lunch becomes a meal eaten with an iPad propped in front of the plate instead of a conversation with a co-worker.

It doesn't take long before entrepreneurs turn their café into their office and start looking for those outlets and Wi-Fi passwords. It doesn't take too long afterwards that they're considering co-working. As well, it won't be long after that before they're looking to rent their own office space, even if it means a commute and a battle for a parking space.

An entrepreneur will understand beforehand that this process of aloneness is going to happen so that they can prepare ahead of time and won't make some poor money management judgments just for comradery. An entrepreneur can find the sociability that all humans need by having lunch meetings, attending events and getting to meet ups. Also, scheduling in significant other time, family time, and exercising with a friend all go a long way toward keeping the entrepreneur mentally healthy and fully focused on their new business venture.

46

You'd Rather Have An Office
Than A Spare Bedroom

afés and co-working spaces will be occasional treats for entrepreneurs in the days and months before their new business outgrows a single desk. But most of an entrepreneur's long hours will be spent not in some noisy coffee house or in a friendly entrepreneurial hub but in their spare bedroom. Rather, in their personal office conveniently located just down the hall from their own bedroom. Given a choice between keeping a spare room for occasional guests or turning an empty room into a place where things get done, entrepreneurs will always find themselves wondering how they're going to get the extra bed out of the house. A spare room is always just a workspace waiting to happen.

There are a number of benefits to making that change. While converting a spare room into an office can require some up-front costs—for a new chair, a new desk, bookshelves and the business books to put on them, and office equipment, it is worth it to note that an office can raise the value of a home.

According to one study conducted by the National Association of Realtors, 44 percent of home buyers were willing to pay nearly $2,000 more for a home with a study, den, home office or library. Keep your expenditures below that cost level in your own home, and building a home office might just be your company's first profit.

On top of that additional value comes rebates. Once you're working from home, you can start deducting some household expenses from your taxes. When you have a clear separation between an office and the rest of the household (a screen or a curtain is clear enough) you can usually make a quick deduction of up to $1,500 per year on your taxes. As soon you start working for yourself, it's definitely worth talking to a tax advisor to make sure that your home office gives you all the deductions it can.

The biggest benefit of growing a business from your upstairs landing, though, isn't the short commute, the extra value of a home with a built-in workspace, or even the extra-extra value of a property that might one day have a plaque saying that it once housed the first office of a global corporation. It's that you're home when the kids come back from school. Really.

Now, that might not sound like an advantage but for entrepreneurs with young families it can feel like a huge advantage. You know you're going to be working long hours. You know that in the first years and certainly the first months of the business, you're going to be working every hour you don't have to waste eating or sleeping.

Your partner might understand that you're not going to be around very much and that a date for an entrepreneur means checking their schedule, making the reservation and pushing the date and time into their Google calendar. The partner also learns to "get it" and be prepared to be stood up when a new customer demands a change at the last moment. That's life with an entrepreneur, and the partner also understands that they will benefit from the great business when all is said and done.

Children don't get it because they don't understand why their parent would rather spend their Saturday's preparing a new A/B test instead of taking them to the park. They don't understand why you're skipping lunch at grandma's house to stay at home and finish the website. They don't understand why you can't help them with their homework, but can write email after email after email to people you don't even know. Being an entrepreneur involves sacrifices. It means that other people have to make sacrifices too, and not all of those people will understand why.

Working from home is one of the few occasions when being an entrepreneur can give back to the family in its first months. There's less of a rush in the morning when you don't have to pack up your work and head to the office before the kids even leave for school, or as soon as the kids are out of the house.

There's no need to ask for time off when one of the children is sick and has to spend the day on the sofa with a bowl of soup and a stack of DVDs. As a bonus, there are fewer feelings of guilt about staying at the office until late when the office is upstairs and you can see your kids every time you head to the kitchen to load up on coffee.

One of the biggest differences between an employee who puts in long hours at the office and an entrepreneur who puts in long hours from their home office is that the entrepreneur gets to work hard and still see their family.

Of course, there's a price to be paid for that stronger family connection. Working in a home filled with children means working in a home filled with disruptions. Telling children that when the office door is closed, their parent is busy and shouldn't be disturbed rarely works. Television might be an entrepreneur's best friend, a way to keep children quiet and in one place while they're finishing a presentation or checking a report, but it has its limits.

Some experts have suggested using color codes on the office door: red mean no interruptions except for emergencies (my mom used to say red meant only bother her if there was blood); yellow means knock and wait; green is the same as the door being open. Giving children specific times when you're available can help too, as long as they don't have to wait too long.

It's not just children who see a parent in a home office as a parent who's available for parenting. While an entrepreneur understands that working from a home office is just a more convenient way to get things done, for other people, working from home sounds as though you're not working at all.

Until you get your own office, you can expect to be asked to run all sorts of favors and complete household chores that might otherwise have been shared. Because your schedule is flexible, it's tempting to agree to do each of these little errands, even though they eat into your working time.

An entrepreneur will find it's not the errand that may only take literally five minutes; it's the break in your concentration. Studies have been done on this interruption topic. Psychologists call the interruption, and the accompanying, get back to work process as "retooling time." The studies show that "retooling" after an interruption takes just about 45 minutes. It won't take more that a few of these interruptions in a day to eat into your valuable time and delay your goal of getting your business up and running and paying off. Again, it's important to set boundaries, otherwise you'll find those potentially long hours start to fill with non-productive time.

If it all gets too much, you can always escape to the café or even the library is a good quiet place.

47

You Don't Scrimp On Sleep, Except At Night

Margaret Thatcher was famous for ignoring the need to sleep, getting by on just four hours a night. (Her husband, Denis, was once heard to shout at her: "Woman — bed!") Other leaders also seem to manage with a minimal amount of shut-eye. Winston Churchill would ease himself into bed at about three in the morning and push himself out five hours later. Marissa Meyer sleeps from midnight until around four or six at the latest. Richard Branson is a little lazier, if you want to call it that: he also knocks off at midnight and rises no later than six but he doesn't wake earlier than five.

According to one limited survey of 21 of the world's most successful people, 14 percent make do with between four and five hours of sleep a night and 32 percent give themselves between five and six hours. Little more than a quarter slept a full seven to eight hours. Asked how much sleep people need, Napoleon Bonaparte is reputed to have answered: "Six for a man, seven for a woman, eight for a fool."

For some people getting by on tiny amounts of sleep might be fine. Some scientists say that they have found a gene that enables some people to sleep for less time than others. The researchers studied 100 sets of twins, depriving them of sleep for 38 hours. They found that one twin with a particular gene mutation had 40 percent fewer lapses of concentration and required just eight hours of sleep to recover. His brother needed nine-and-a-half hours.

The finding is debatable. More studies have documented the damage that lack of sleep can cause. Cognitive performance declines, particularly when long or monotonous tasks must be done, and perceptive skills become blunter even as the subjects continue to overestimate their abilities. When we do without sleep, we perform worse, but we still believe we're doing fine. Charles Moore, Margaret Thatcher's official biographer, agreed that the late British Prime Minister could work longer hours than most but says that she needed more sleep than she believed.

For entrepreneurs, those sleep surveys should be a concern. Margaret Thatcher has been gone for a few years now and her distinguished career as Prime Minister ended in 1990. Bonaparte has been deceased somewhat longer, and there would be little debate that he didn't have today's stress to make the need for sleep even more concerning.

No one is more aware that hours spent asleep are not hours spent being productive, than people who own their own businesses. Lying in bed and dreaming might be enjoyable and relaxing, but it doesn't get the presentation finished, and you can't read or write a white paper in your sleep, no matter how much you might think you can.

Those quiet hours in the middle of the night when the world is asleep and the phone is unlikely to ring can be the best time to focus and get things done. And the same is true of the early morning. Rise before the sun is up (or at least before the emails start to come in) and you might be able to add an extra hour of productivity to the day.

But, there's a price, and that price is usually larger than the value of the extra work you're able to get done. When sleep falls below six hours a night, you can expect to find yourself making more mistakes, taking longer to complete simple tasks, and finding it harder to concentrate for longer periods.

Not that that's going to stop you. It's one thing to know that tomorrow you might struggle to get all the way through a report you need to read without dozing off; it's another thing altogether when the clock strikes midnight, the house is silent and you've got a pile of data in front of you that's revealing all sorts of interesting trends.

Even if you wanted to go to bed at ten and wake up fully refreshed at six, you'd struggle to do so. Often entrepreneurs find that they never really rest. Even when an entrepreneur is vegetating in front of the television (rare) in the evening, and their partner has forbidden them to touch their phone or iPad, sadly, the entrepreneur brains are still running and churning through all of the tasks that can be completed when the show is over and they are going over in their minds the meetings that are coming up tomorrow.

It's hard enough for an entrepreneur to sit still. It's almost impossible for an entrepreneur's brain to stop thinking. Climb into bed and it doesn't matter how tired you might feel, your brain is going to keep rolling through options and decisions and ideas for hours until it eventually dozes off.

Tim Ferriss, author of productivity book, *The Four-Hour Workweek*, has talked about his own insomnia and laid out solutions that include a couple of tablespoons of peanut butter before bedtime, cold baths (I say hot) and sleeping in the half-military crawl position. In practice, entrepreneurs are more likely to find themselves lying in bed, staring at the ceiling and thinking through solutions to marketing and product problems.

It's true that entrepreneurs burn the candle at both ends. They go to bed late and they wake up early, and for months the most familiar emotion they feel is fatigue. The way they beat that fatigue isn't to find a way to squeeze the traditional eight hours sleep into an entrepreneurial lifestyle—which just doesn't exactly fit. The solution is generally to assume that this period isn't going to last forever. It's to burn for a few months to get to the launch or land some funding.

During that time, entrepreneurs will work all the hours they can, including those hours when other people are sleeping. They'll catch up by sleeping a little later on the weekends, and they'll doze off during cinema dates or while their partner binge-watches Netflix. Sometimes they'll even shut the office door, close their eyes and crash at (or under) their desk for twenty minutes.

However, you can train yourself into better sleeping habits. And don't fool yourself, it means training—real training. While the training may be more difficult when you are just starting out with your product or service, or you have just quit your day job, it is worth the effort to know how to sleep when you have to so that you don't spend hours lying there with your mind churning.

48

You Have An App For Everything

You have to take your hat off to people who started their businesses back in the days when people actually wore hats. They might have had sleek designs in their offices and real secretaries to screen their calls but they didn't have smartphones. Or tablets. Or even computers. Doing without email probably helped them to work a bit faster and the martini lunches might have been fun, even if they weren't very productive, but it's hard for any entrepreneur nowadays to imagine creating a business without the help of the smartphone and all the apps it contains.

What a drill is to the road working crews and a rocket is to an astronaut—that's what the smartphone has become for an entrepreneur. It's the Swiss (or Cupertino) army knife that can crack open any task and ensure rising efficient productivity. And bonus, the phone can even be used to make phone calls!

Every entrepreneur has their own collection of favorite apps and it's always fun to compare home screens with other business builders to see if they have any apps you've missed. But even if the apps themselves differ, there are some tasks that every entrepreneur now turns to their phone to solve.

A synchronized **Calendar**, for example, is essential and not just to jot down meeting times and birthdays. You can add premade calendars that show public holidays in different countries, sports schedules and even stardates. By allowing other people access to your calendar, you can avoid date clashes. When every minute is precious, entrepreneurs have been known to tell family members to schedule times for quick phone calls. On a smartphone it's as basic as a dial pad.

Other apps are less essential but you're still going to find them, or a version of them, on just about every entrepreneur's smartphone. **Camcard** is a business card reader. Even in the age of Facetime, LinkedIn and synchable contact lists, bits of thick paper with your name, title and business name are still an essential part of an entrepreneur's toolkit. You'll hand them out like confetti, complete with a Snapchat code, at business conferences, and know that the piece of card will soon be discarded but the information will be scanned into the person's phone.

Tripit is an easy way to make and keep track of travel plans. It focuses on the essential information on your plane ticket to produce an itinerary that's easy to see and simple to follow. It's a lot more efficient than keeping folders of confirmation emails or trying to use your iPhone's Wallet app. Tripit certainly isn't the only travel app available, of course. Others include **TripCase**, which does much the same thing as Tripit; **Roomer**, which can help to find hotel rooms; and **Google Flights** and **SkyScanner** to track down cheap flights. The moment you find yourself flying at conferences and business meetings, you'll find yourself downloading one of them and regarding the app as essential.

You'll also want to keep track of your staff while you're on the road, or your freelancers if your company is still mostly virtual. **Flowdock** is one collaboration tool that combines chat and inbox functions but there are plenty of others, including **Trello**, **Asana**, and of course, **Dropbox**, **Google Docs**, and **Skype**. Again, whichever apps you choose, you'll find that you're able to manage an entire team strung around the world with nothing more than the touch of an app on the smartphone and of course, an entry on a shared calendar.

One of the strangest apps that an entrepreneur can use, and one of the most addictive apps once it's placed on a tablet computer, is **Splashtop**. Together with a small program downloaded onto a computer, it turns the tablet into a remote control for your laptop. You can sit in your living room and open your work in progress on the computer in the office. It means you don't have to carry your computer around with you wherever you go, and it can always access your work wherever you are. It puts the entire office in your pocket.

Those are just the most essential apps, and you can add to them the various to-do lists and reminder apps, social media apps, audiobooks, memos and voice recorders for when you get an idea as you're driving along. In short, there's an app for whatever an entrepreneur might need to do on their tablets or smartphones, and entrepreneurs eventually discover all of them.

If there isn't an app for something an entrepreneur needs to do, there's an opportunity to build one! The rise of the app market, with all its limitations and challenges, has been one of the most significant advances for entrepreneurs since the joint stock company.

Now anyone can build a software product for a relatively low cost, and make it available for anyone to buy and use. While the marketing might not be as simple as it used to be in the early days of the iPhone (when apps like, well, iFart were able to top the charts), a bit of creativity can still go far. Rovio did tremendously well with Angry Birds by focusing its efforts on first reaching the top of the charts in small, overlooked markets such as Greece. That allowed people to start talking about the game, and the rest is a multibillion dollar history.

The challenge for entrepreneurs isn't just to look for opportunities on their smartphones or to use these phones to create more productively, those opportunities are already being exploited to the great benefit for the entrepreneur. The challenge is to remember that there is a life outside the screen, and far more opportunities that can be enjoyed with more than a couple of thumbs. Entrepreneurs spend far more time in front of different-sized screens than most of the population. It's vital to lift your head from those screens, look around and see the chances and the people that exist outside the app stores.

49

You Understand That Time Is
More Valuable Than Money

In 2015, the Freelancers Union put the number of freelancers in the U.S. at around 54 million. More than half of those freelancers had made the jump by choice, a percentage that had increased by 7 percent over the previous year. That's 54 million people working on their own terms, doing their own thing and building their own businesses.

Most of those freelancers will remain freelancers. They won't make the jump to entrepreneurship by looking for ways to scale their business. When their schedule is full, they'll tell new clients that they will have to wait for their work to be taken on. When a freelancer tries to picture where they'll be five or ten years from now, they'll see themselves doing the same thing but perhaps doing better projects for bigger clients and for higher fees. They will always be sole proprietorships, never growing beyond the office in the spare bedroom.

And, that's fine—even, great.

Those freelancers have made the decision that their time is best spent doing the work that they love. That's how they want to fill their days and it's what gives them the greatest fulfillment. Entrepreneurs have a different view of their time. What matters most to entrepreneurs isn't the hours they spend planning sales strategies or figuring out the design of a landing page. It's the result of those efforts.

When an entrepreneur looks forward five or ten years, they see themselves running a large corporation or having sold a large corporation, they will be building their next business, investing in the ideas of other entrepreneurs or even just relaxing on the beach of their private Caribbean island.

For entrepreneurs, work isn't about how they fill their hours. It's about how they build their vision in their heads. Time is the container in which they put those efforts. Money is a motivation but the challenge and the accomplishment are much more powerful incentives.

At the end of the day, a freelancer can count the number of billable hours they worked and estimate the value of the day they've just completed. For entrepreneurs, the amount earned in a particular hour or a particular day or even a particular year doesn't matter. What matters is how much closer those hours brought them to the achievement of their goal.

The moment an entrepreneur realizes that time is about progress not income, time acquires a very different value. There's a myriad of different ways to earn money and some of those ways will produce large sums of cash. If an entrepreneur were only interested in being rich, they would have studied finance or banking and looked for a job with a Wall Street hedge fund. If they had wanted a more reliable career, they could have studied law, medicine or accountancy, all of which would have given them a stable and decent standard of living.

But, for an entrepreneur, a sense of achievement doesn't come from income alone; they understand that a good income might not happen for a long time. Money isn't enough and it doesn't come close to the importance of an hour well-spent.

More importantly, entrepreneurs understand that while there are lots of different way of earning large sums of money, there's no way to earn more time. Nothing they do can give them more than their allotted hours and it doesn't matter how successful their business will be or how rich they might become, they'll have no more years than anyone else. Steve Jobs, for all his wealth and success didn't make it past 56 years of age.

The moment you outsource a task that you could have done yourself, you show that you've made that leap from freelancer or sole proprietor to a genuine entrepreneur. You show that you understand that time is precious and limited, something that can't be made or multiplied. You'll never have more time than you have now. The only thing you can do is to make sure that you're using your time wisely.

Entrepreneurs pay others to free up time to do the tasks that might not bring the greatest wealth but which can bring them the fastest progress. Instead of spending weeks designing a website themselves, they pay someone to build it for them even though money is short and budgets will be tight. (And they pay the full price; sites like Fiverr are a cheap gamble that can either produce a lucky hit or time lost redoing substandard work over and over again.)

So their business grows. One freelancer becomes a couple of employees, then a team and a department. Two departments. Soon you have a payroll and middle management. You have a growing business.

Tim Ferriss's advice to outsource everything might have taken the idea to an extreme but the principle is one used by every successful entrepreneur. To be fair, Ferriss has not given us a way, yet, to outsource our exercise workout, but many ideas in his book are worth incorporating for your own work week.

Look at the desk of a successful business leader and you won't see piles of paper and often you won't even see a computer terminal. The work that they demand is done in other offices. The entrepreneur has outsourced everything so that even the day-to-day management is performed by the Chief of Operations. These leaders are left to make the big decisions that can only be made at the very top.

In an interview with the BBC, President Obama noted that all his decisions are difficult. The easy decisions are made long before they reach his level. The career of an entrepreneur is steady progress towards that job, the one in which their time is spent doing only the tasks that no one else can do and making the decisions for which only they can claim responsibility.

The biggest difference between an entrepreneur and everyone else is the understanding that there's no time to spend all the money they can earn. It's that understanding that turns sole proprietors into business owners and gives them the life they want.

50

You're Not Thinking About Doing It.
You're Doing It

One of the first questions we ask someone when we meet them for the first time is, "What do you do?" It's not exactly that question that we really want to know. What we really want to know is, "Who are you? *What* are you? What kind of person am I talking to? What gives you a sense of passion? What interests you? What do you value and how do you treat others? Where are you guiding your life?"

That's a lot of questions, too many to ask while shaking someone's hand and too difficult for most people to answer, so we ask the one question whose answer encapsulates most of those answers. We ask what someone actually *does*.

It's a question that goes right to the point, and generally tells us everything we need to know.

We could ask a different question. We could ask someone, "Who do you *think* you are?" We could ask them how they see themselves or what they think they could do instead of what they are actually doing. But we don't judge people according to what they think or believe. We judge them by their actions. It's how someone behaves that matters. It's what they do and have done and what they accomplish that counts.

If someone answers that question by saying, "I'm an actor," the next question we would ask would likely be something about where we might have seen them? Even if this individual is mostly waiting tables while waiting for their big break, we'd expect to be told about local theater performances, cable television commercials or even shows.

We'd expect that someone who calls themselves an "actor" is actually *doing* some form of acting, even if they're not yet living in Beverly Hills and playing lead roles in action movies. Similarly, if someone says they're a lawyer, we'd ask about the sort of law they practice or where they went to law school. We'd certainly be surprised if they replied that they're currently serving coffee drinks in Starbucks, but they're thinking of applying to law school in the next year or two—maybe. We might even be tempted to correct them by pointing out that they're *thinking* of becoming a lawyer. They're not a lawyer, yet.

The same principle applies to entrepreneurs.

Throughout this book, we've described characteristics that show that someone *is* an entrepreneur. We've talked about where entrepreneurs come from and where they want to go. We've talked about the people they surround themselves with and the personality traits that make up the entrepreneurial spirit. Whether those traits are what push someone to become an entrepreneur or the traits are what develops once an entrepreneur starts building their own business isn't important. The traits will generally be found in every entrepreneur, and they're part of what drives someone to build a company.

We've also talked about the entrepreneurial way of life. But what all of these characteristics have in common is that they're actions.

Everyone has ideas. Everyone has solved the world's biggest problems while they brushed their teeth in the morning or sat on the subway watching the stations pass. Everyone has thought of a concept that could earn billions and change the world. Ideas are cheap. In fact, they're free.

Actions are tough, and they require effort, usually in the form of sacrifice.

Actions, effort, and sacrifice are not magic, but they are adjectives that describe what makes an entrepreneur.

Entrepreneurs are willing to pay that price. They take action. They quit their jobs or having been fired for acting more like an entrepreneur than an employee, they stop looking for a new and different job. They devote hours to writing a business plan just like a road map so that they will know exactly where they are heading and what they're going to be doing all along the way. Or they may lock themselves away for weeks, as Nick Woodman of GoPro did, while they build their prototype product.

They prepare their pitches and work their contacts so that they can persuade investors to give them the cash they need to hire staff and buy advertising. They bet and invest their own money in their ideas, hiring people to work for them so that they can spend their hours where they're most needed.

Entrepreneurship is a state of being. An entrepreneur is a type of person, a unique, rare kind, the kind that creates jobs, builds industries and keeps the economy moving. Entrepreneurs are visionaries and dreamers, courageous and generous, and they change the world.

They provide the places that allow people who aren't entrepreneurs to do the work that *they* love and to find the fulfillment they desire. The entrepreneur pays their taxes, sponsors events and supports towns.

They draw employees into areas so that communities can be formed and thrive and grow.

Entrepreneurs are at the heart of everything that society needs to be prosperous.

Above all, entrepreneurs are doers. They're people of action. They're people for whom a good idea is a start and a concept is the beginning of a plan. They understand that an idea on its own is meaningless. What matters is the work.

A good idea has to be built. A plan has to be implemented. The risks have to be taken, the hours have to be filled, the staff have to be hired and the tests have to be run, then rerun, then run again. An entrepreneur is someone who, while continuing to think and dream, actually breaks a sweat.

How do you know you're an entrepreneur? When you meet someone and shake their hand, and they ask what you do, you know you are an entrepreneur because you start your answer by saying, "I have a company that does..." or "I run a business that does..." or "I'm building a prototype that does..." And, whatever "it" does, you are the one *doing* that "it." The operative word is, "doing."

When you're building your business—at whatever stage and whatever size—and that business is what defines you, you know you're an entrepreneur.

About the Authors

Joel Comm is an author, speaker, consultant and entrepreneur with 12 published books. These books include *The AdSense Code, Click Here to Order: Stories from the World's Most Successful Entrepreneurs, KaChing: How to Run an Online Business that Pays and Pays and Twitter Power 2.0.* He has also written over 40 ebooks. He has appeared in *The New York Times,* on Jon Stewart's The Daily Show, on CNN online, on Fox News, and many other places.

John Rampton is an entrepreneur who has started and sold a number of successful businesses and currently operates Due, an online invoice and payments company. He has had a successful blog that is followed by thousands and has turned into an influencer in entrepreneurism, technology, and Internet Marketing. John has also spoken at many technology, marketing, and entrepreneur events.

Morgan James
Speakers Group

↗ www.TheMorganJamesSpeakersGroup.com

We connect Morgan James published authors with live and online events and audiences whom will benefit from their expertise.

Morgan James makes all of our titles available
through the Library for All Charity Organization.

www.LibraryForAll.org